AIR FRYER
COOKBOOK
WITH PICTURES

Amazingly Easy & Healthy Air Fryer Recipes to Fry, Bake, Grill
& Roast, for Beginners & Advanced
Users. Even for One & Two

SAGE COOKE

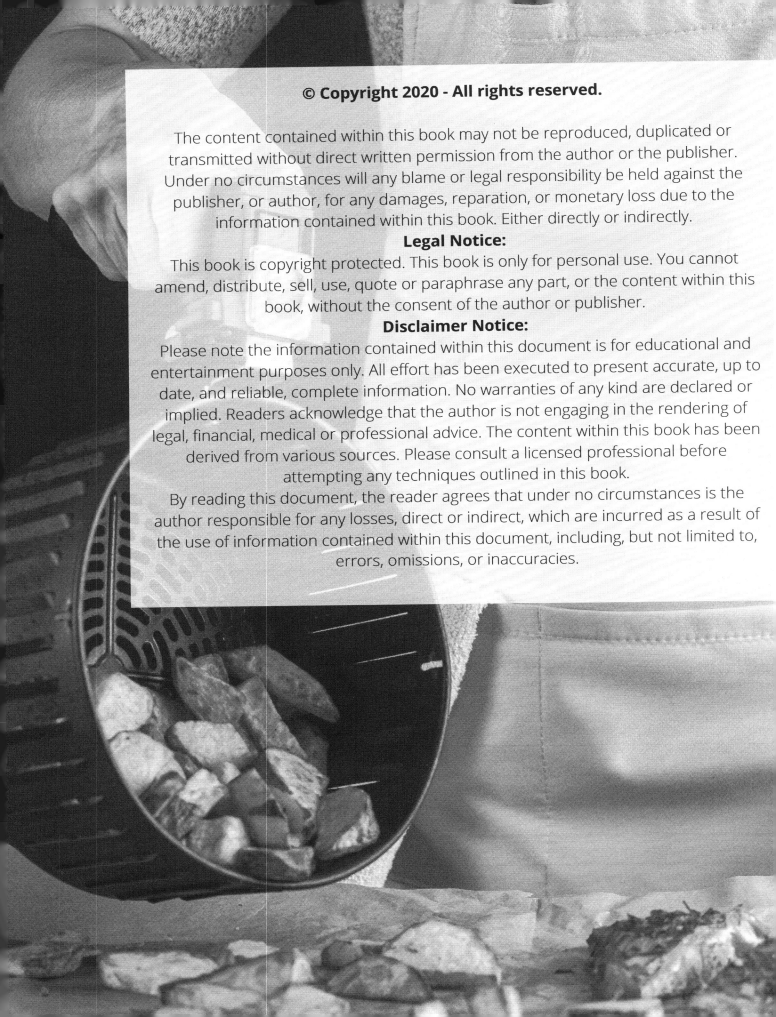

CONTENTS

Introduction

AIR FRYER RECIPES

Introduction

We all know the fantastic taste of deep-fried foods. In fact, the mere mention of deep-fried beef burgers, French fries, chicken drumsticks is mouth-watering. Whether you are a home cook or a skillful chef, you will concur that deep-frying food is one of the efficient, convenient, and most used cooking methods.

However, we can't deny that deep-fried food is unhealthy. They are highly packed with calories and fat that significantly affects our health. Also, deep-frying ingredients lose vital nutrients and, even worse, expose our bodies to the risk of cancer, obesity, and diabetes despite their flavor full taste.

Fortunately, the cooking revolution began with the introduction of the air fryer. You can now cook crunchy, crispy meals and protect your family, without compromising flavor and without the hefty clean-up and expenses associated with deep frying. Even better, you can achieve better results since your food is super crispy with little or no oil.

The promise of this kitchen gadget is simple; Crunchy, healthy food. It can make guilt-free French fries, nachos, lamb roasts in half the time you make them in the oven. It can also cook strip steak in less time it takes to preheat a grill and can reheat leftovers producing better results than your microwave.

Too good to be true. Right? This cookbook is going to be your torchbearer. It will guide you into understanding and mastering how the air fryer works, tips and tricks of using the air fryer, troubleshooting it, and delicious recipes for almost every occasion with easy-to-follow steps and beautiful photos of the result.
You will get the secrets to making the most of your Air Fryer and not feel guilty for having forgotten it in an unused corner of the kitchen. It won't happen!

Thanks to this Guide, as soon as you taste your dishes, you will not believe your eyes. You will feel the King of the kitchen. Family and friends will be thrilled by the goodness of your dishes!

What are you waiting for? Let's go!

WELCOME!

How does it work?

An air fryer is an amp-ed-up small counter-top convection oven that stimulates deep frying food without submerging them in oil. It cooks food using heating elements accompanied by a powerful fan that circularly swirls hot air in the cooking chamber. The hot air reaches the ingredients creating a crispy crust on the outside and a moist inside.

What makes an air fryer so good at its job is the perforated basket. This is where the food sits. The perforations help increase the contact between food and the moving hot air.

Let's have an overview of how to use an air fryer

1.Place the food in the perforated basket.

The size of the basket varies with the air fryer size. The basket may hold 2-10 quarts of ingredients. It's recommended to add 1-2 tablespoons of oil to achieve fried foods' crunchiness.

2.Set the desired time and temperature

Air fryer times range from 5-25 minutes, while the temperature ranges from 350 F-400F.

3.Give the food time to cook.

It's highly recommended to flip the food halfway through the cooking time, which helps the food crisp up evenly.

Benefits of using the air fryer

1.May aid weight loss

The key to successful weight loss is watching the eating and cooking habits. The air fryer reduces calorie intake and may contribute to weight loss. Besides, the air fryer uses a tablespoon or no oil, thus reduces fattening cholesterol intake.

2.Safe to use.

Unlike deep frying that involves heating a large amount of oil that may spill or splash, posing an accident, the air fryer uses a little or no oil. The air fryer comes with auto shutdown features when the cooking cycle is complete, preventing it from overheating and burning. Even better, the air fryer has non-slip feet that ensure the appliance doesn't slip when cooking causing accidents.

3. Cooks food faster

Foods cook fast in the air fryer than other kitchen appliances such as the oven. The air fryers also do not require preheating before cooking commences. Most importantly, you may transfer frozen ingredients from the freezer straight to the air fryer.

4.Perfect for veggies picky eaters

Air frying vegetables such as broccoli, kale, or Brussels sprouts are great solutions for picky vegetable eaters. The veggies come out crispy and tastier, thus irresistible. Moreover, some air fryer recipes give bread and vegetables before air frying, incorporating healthy options such as chickpeas and rice crumbs.

5.Easy to clean

Not only is it easy to cook with an air fryer but also to clean. Most of the removable components of the air fryer are dishwasher safe. You can also soak them in warm soapy water or wipe them with a damp cloth.

6.It takes less of your kitchen space.

If you have a small kitchen space, this is a perfect kitchen appliance for you. It takes up less of the counter-top space and is sleek, thus a great addition to the kitchen. The air fryer also doesn't leave your house with fried food smells that last for hours after cooking.

Tips and tricks of using the air fryer

An air fryer can be a great addition to your kitchen if you use it in the right way. Below are some tips to help you exploit its full potential.

Preparing to Air Fry

1.Ensure that your air fryer is placed on a stable and level counter-top that is heat resistant. You should also leave at least 5 inches distance between a surface and the air fryer exhaust vent.

2. It's unnecessary, but it is advisable to preheat the air fryer before adding the ingredients. Set the timer for 2-3 minutes and add food immediately; the timer stops.

3.Invest in a hand-pumped kitchen cooking spray bottle. Spraying oil on the food is better than brushing or drizzling. Less oil is used and reaches the ingredients evenly. However, be aware of oil cans with aerosol agents that can corrode your air fryer basket non-stick surface.

4.Use an aluminum sling to remove the air fryer's hot cooking accessories. Fold a piece of aluminum foil into a sling of about 21/2" wide and 25 long. Please place it in the air fryer and the baking dish on it, and then tuck in the ends in the basket. Once the cooking cycle is complete, untuck the sling and lift the baking dish.

5.Invest in the right air fryer accessories. You may purchase brand new ones or may already have some. Let's say, for example; you have an oven-safe baking dish. It can also be used in the air fryer as long as they fit in the appliance and don't touch the heating element.

6.If your recipe involves breading, make sure to use the proper breading technique. Coat the ingredients with flour, then dip in the egg and finally in crumbs. Press the crumbs using your hands to ensure they are not brown off by the fan.

When Air Frying

1.Fatty foods, e.g., bacon and meat burgers, produce grease that tends to smoke when too hot. Therefore, add cold water to the drawer below the air fryer basket to prevent the grease from getting hot and smoking.

2.Just like you would, when cooking on the stovetop, grill, or skillet, flip food halfway through the cooking cycle. You can also shake the air fryer basket during the cooking cycle to distribute the ingredients well. This helps crisping, browning, and cooking evenly.

3.We tend to overcrowd the skillet or other cooking appliances, so why not the air fryer? I can't stress this enough. Overcrowding the basket to cook more at a time will prevent food from cooking and crisping well.

4.Unlike some cooking appliances, you can check the food doneness as often as it's required and as you like. This is the most exciting part of using the air fryer since you don't interrupt the timing. Some air fryer models continue heating even when the drawer is open, while others pick from where it left off once the drawer is returned.

5.Secure light food like the top bun on a sandwich with a toothpick to avoid them being blown around by the powerful fan.

6.Spray your food halfway through the cooking cycle to get it brownier and crispier

7.Cook food without overlapping. This helps plenty of air circulation, attributing to even cooking. However, you can stack vegetables, e.g., Brussels sprouts, and flip them a few times during the cooking process.

8.Always use a meat thermometer on meat to ensure the meat browns nicely on the outside and reach the inside's proper temperature.

After Air frying

1.Remove the air fryer basket from the drawer before pouring food on a serving platter. This prevents you from pouring excess grease and fat alongside the air-fried food.

2.Do not pour the cooking juices from the drawer just yet. The drawer catches marinade from cooking food packed with flavor and may be used as a serving sauce. If the liquid is too thin, boil it over the stove-top until it thickens. You may also add cornstarch and cook it over the stove-top for a few minutes to thicken. Serve the air-fried food with the gravy.

3.After using the air fryer, clean the basket and the drawer with warm soapy water. Return the accessories and turn on the air fryer for 3 minutes to dry itself. This ensures the accessories are well dried compared to using towels.

Valuable tools to exploit all potential of the air fryer

Did you just purchase your first air fryer? Are you wondering what to do with it? If either or both questions answer is yes, here are essential accessories to get you started with your air fryer. The tools will make it easy for you to make almost everything in your air fryer.

Silicone locking tongs

Tongs are used to move food in and out of the air fryer, protecting your fingers and arms from burns. Ensure the tongs are flexible, heat resistant, dishwasher safe, stainless, and has silicon heads to grip food easily.

Air fryer liners

Invest in non-stick and non-toxic air fryer liners. They prevent food from sticking and keeps fatty residue out, making cleaning up a breeze.

Reversible Air fryer Rack

Air fryers perform great work circulating air around your food in the air fryer. However, large foods such as beef roast or chicken drumsticks will require an elevation so that the air can circulate them evenly instead of leaving one side of the food to lie on the air fryer bottom. Even better, some racks come with skewers for vegetable or meat kabobs and peach bourbon wings. The rack is also dishwasher safe, thus easy to clean up.

Air fryer Silicon Cups

The reusable silicone cups are used to create muffin cups, cupcakes, or egg cups. They help create batches of similar foods or personalized foods at once in the air fryer.

Air fryer grill pan

When it comes to cooking fish or other meat, an air fryer grill pan is a convenient tool you must have. It comes with a perforated surface to allow air circulation. It is also non-stick and dishwasher safe for easy cleaning.

Air fryer baking pan

As aforementioned, the air fryer resembles a convection oven, thus great for baking. The baking pan fits in the air fryer and can cook all sorts of baked foods ranging from cakes, bread, eggs with vegetables, macaroni and cheese, pizza, among others.

Mandoline slicer

Do you love air-fried French fries, onion rings, or sliced pickles? Mandoline is the one for you. This pull and slice equipment has different thickness settings to choose from as per the recipe requirement. Remember to follow mandoline safety precautions to avoid injuries.

Spray Bottle

Spraying your food is the secret to crispier and brownier food in the air fryer. It's also economical to spray oil compared to brushing or drizzling oil on the food. We earlier stated that some oil cans contain aerosol agents that can dissipate your air fryer coating. Right? Fill a spray bottle with your favourite oil before air frying for an excellent food outcome and a lasting relationship with your air fryer.

Meat Thermometer

Correct cooking times and food temperatures are the key to successful air frying. A meat thermometer ensures your food is cooked up to the proper temperatures. The thermometer can read the food temperatures within seconds and be folded and stored anywhere.

Maintenance and troubleshooting

You were excited that you finally got your dream magical kitchen appliance. You even told your friends and invited them over to your place to witness how you are now making and eating healthy. You feel very proud of yourself and can't ask for more. Sadly, after some time, the air fryer doesn't work right. There must be something wrong with it. You are now wondering how to deal with it and get your air fryer back on track. Below are some problems common with air fryers and their solutions.

Problem: The smell of old food
Remedy:
Foods with strong smells such as fish or bacon may leave an odor in your air fryer. The perfect way to deal with the odors is to clean the air fryer immediately after you are done with cooking. If the smell persists, soak the basket and the drawer in warm soapy water for about an hour, clean them again. Suppose that doesn't work half a lemon and rub the halves over the accessories. Let sit for half an hour and wash with soapy water. The air fryer should now be clean and smell fresh.

Problem: The air fryer won't switch on or off
Remedy:
This is a common issue among many air fryers and is the easiest to fix. The air fryer's main reason for failing to switch on is a wrongly plugged power source. Counter-check the air fryer connection and fit it well. Another main reason is an overloaded socket limiting the amount of power reaching your gadget. If this is the case, unplug some devices from the socket; otherwise, use an alternative idle socket for the air fryer.

Problem: White Smoke
Remedy:
White smoke is mostly not smoke but steam that naturally occurs when cooking moist food. If the smoke has a smell, unplug the air fryer immediately. Check if there is accumulated grease on the drip pan resulting from cooking fatty foods. If that is the case, let the air fryer cool and wash the grease.

Problem: Black smoke
Remedy:
Black smoke is the result of cooking fatty foods at high temperatures. The smoke may produce an odor of burning fat. You can prevent this by adding a small amount of water to the basket's bottom, where hot oil will land and cool.

Problem: Blue smoke
Remedy:

Blue smoke is exceptionally rare but a cause for concern. If it does happen, it means that there is an electric problem. You should act fast, unplug the air fryer, and don't plug it back until a technician attends it. If you don't desire to repair the air fryer consider purchasing a new air fryer.

Problem: Food lacks a crispy finish
Remedy:

The lack of a crispy texture in your air fried is commonly observed when your food cooks with air instead of oil. Always spray cooking spray on the ingredients before air frying.

Problem: Improperly cooked food
Remedy:

This is a common predicament among many air fryer users. It's mainly caused by overloading the basket leading to the hot air not reaching all the food. This can be solved by cooking small batches of food and shaking the basket regularly to help distribute heat evenly.

Problem: Air fryer not blowing hot air
Remedy:

Failure of an air fryer to blow hot air is a fault that should be repaired by the manufacturer or the outlet where you bought the appliance. If your warranty has not yet expired, ensure to get a repair service.

Problem: producing too much noise
Remedy:

If your air fryer is making a rattling noise, it's most likely an accessory or a part inside is not well fitted. You can correct this by switching it off cleaning it while inspecting if there is any tightening needed in the interior. Moreover, if the fan is moving at a very high speed, it is likely to make noise as loud as the noise made by a vacuum.

Problem: Air fryer peeling
Remedy:

If your air fryer non-stick surface starts to peel weeks or a month after purchase, it is a call for action. You may be using abrasive cleaning equipment or using a can of oil with aerosol agents. Prevent such incidents by cleaning the air fryer with a soft sponge and purchase a spray bottle.

FAQ

What food can you make in the air fryer?

The list of foods the air fryer can make is endless. If you love veggies cooked differently or are a picky vegetable eater, cooking them in the air fryer will amaze you. You can also make muffins, seafood, chicken, mashed potatoes, French fries in the most remarkable way. Frozen foods are another addition to the list of foods an air fryer can make. However, they will be cooked for longer times than fresh foods. Last but not least, Instead of microwaving leftovers try air frying them and thank me later.

Are Air fryers healthy?

The air fryer uses hot air instead of oil, making it a healthy option. Air frying reduces calories and cholesterol intake, unlike deep frying food and other cooking methods. You are aware of the adverse effects of deep-fried foods ranging from obesity, thrombosis, and cancer, which can be avoided by eating similar crunch food cooked by the air fryer.

Is an air fryer better than an oven?

This is a tricky question to answer. Both the air fryer and the oven have their pros and cons. The air fryer saves time and allows different cooking techniques to make unique dishes. On the other hand, an oven cooks delicious food in large quantities. Therefore, it would be fair to say no appliance is better than the other, and they just perform their roles to perfection differently.

Can I use aluminum foil in the air fryer?

Yes, you can. However, it would be best if you did not place it at the bottom of the air fryer where grease accumulates, thus interrupting airflow. This may impact how the air fryer works. Also, the foil should not hang beyond the basket edges or lay in the air fryer without food.

Can I add more ingredients when cooking?

Yes, add as many ingredients as you desire. However, it would help if you were swift to avoid heat loss, thus increasing the cooking time. You can also check for food doneness when cooking.

With that, I hope you find the answer to your query on this magic kitchen appliance.

BREAKFAST

AIR FRYER FRITTATA

Preparation Time: 15 minutes
Cooking time: 20 minutes
Serving: 2

Ingredients
- Cooking spray
- ¼ lb fully cooked and crumbled sausage
- 4 eggs, beaten
- ½ cup Cheddar-Monterrey jack cheese blend, shredded
- 2 tbsp diced green bell pepper
- 1 chopped green onion
- 1 pinch cayenne pepper

Directions
1. Preheat the air fryer to 360°F and spray a cake pan with cooking spray.
2. Mix all the ingredients in a bowl until they are well combined.
3. Transfer the mixture in the bowl to the cake pan.
4. Cook the frittata for 20 minutes.
5. Transfer the frittata to a serving platter.
6. Serve and enjoy.

Nutrition- Per Serving: Calories 381kcal, Total Fat:27g, Carbs: 3g, Proteins 31g

Variation: The sausage can be replaced with leftover steak.

AIR FRYER BLUEBERRY MUFFINS

Preparation Time: 10 minutes
Cooking time: 15 minutes
Serving: 12

Ingredients
- 1 ½ cups all-purpose flour
- ¾ cup oatmeal
- ½ tbsp salt
- ½ tbsp cinnamon
- ½ cup brown sweetener
- 1 tbsp baking powder
- ½ cup of milk
- 2 eggs, beaten
- 2 tbsp vanilla
- ¼ cup unsalted butter, melted
- 1 cup blueberries

Directions
1. In a bowl, mix the flour, oatmeal, salt, cinnamon, brown sweetener, and baking powder.
2. In a separate bowl, whisk the milk, eggs, vanilla, and butter.
3. Stir in the dry ingredients to the wet ingredients.
4. Add the blueberries to the batter and mix.
5. Preheat the air fryer to 351°F.
6. Transfer the batter to 12 silicone muffin cups.
7. Cook the muffins for 15 minutes.
8. Serve and enjoy.

Nutrition- Per Serving: Calories 11kcal, Total Fat:11g, Carbs: 11g, Proteins 11g

Variation: Brown sugar can be used instead of brown sweetener.

Fresh or frozen blueberries can be used depending on your preference.

AIR FRYER SWEET POTATO SKINS

Preparation Time: 7 minutes
Cooking time: 23 minutes
Serving: 4
Ingredients

- 2 sweet potatoes
- 2 tbsp olive oil
- Salt to taste
- 4 eggs, beaten
- ¼ cup whole milk
- pepper to taste
- 4 bacon slices, cooked
- ¼ cup cheddar cheese, grated
- 2 sliced green onions

Directions

1. Wash the sweet potatoes and cook them in a microwave for 8 minutes until they are soft.
2. Wear the oven mitt and slice the sweet potatoes lengthwise into halves.
3. Scoop most of the sweet potato flesh leaving ¼ inch thick flesh.
4. Brush the sweet potato skins with oil and sprinkle them with salt.
5. Preheat the air fryer to 399°F.
6. Place the sweet potato skins in the air fryer and cook them for 10 minutes.
7. Meanwhile, mix the eggs, milk, salt, and pepper in a skillet.
8. Cook the egg mixture for about 2 minutes over medium heat stirring constantly.
9. Top the sweet potato skins with 2 spoonfuls of the egg mixture and 1 slice of bacon.
10. Cover the sweet potato with cheese and cook in the air fryer for 3 minutes.
11. Garnish the sweet potato skins with green onion and serve.

Nutrition- Per Serving: Calories 207kcal, Total Fat:12g, Carbs: 15g, Proteins 11g
Variation: The desired type of cheese can be used.

AIR FRYER OMELETTE

Preparation Time: 2 minutes
Cooking time: 10 minutes
Serving: 4
Ingredients

- 2 eggs, beaten
- ¼ cup milk
- Salt to taste
- ¼ cup fresh meat, minced
- ½ red bell pepper, diced
- 1 green onion, diced
- ½ cup fresh mushroom, diced
- 4 tbsp garden herb
- ¼ cup mozzarella cheese, shredded

Directions

1. Whisk the eggs and milk in a bowl.
2. Stir in salt, meat, and veggies to the egg mixture.
3. Pour the egg mixture into a greased pan.
4. Place the pan in an air fryer basket and cook at 351°F for about 5 minutes.
5. Sprinkle the garden herb onto the omelet then sprinkle it with cheese.
6. Cook the omelet for 5 minutes.
7. Transfer the omelet to a serving platter.
8. Serve and enjoy.

Nutrition- Per Serving: Calories 106kcal, Total Fat:6g, Carbs: 5g, Proteins 10g

Variation: The garden herb can be replaced with the desired seasoning.

AIR FRYER SAUSAGE AND CHEESE WRAPS

Preparation Time: 5 minutes
Cooking time: 6 minutes
Serving: 8

Ingredients
- 8 Heat N' Serve sausage
- 2 pieces American Cheese, sliced
- 8 refrigerated crescent roll dough
- 8 wooden skewers

Directions
1. Separate the crescent roll dough into triangles on a flat surface.
2. Place one triangle on a flat surface and place the sausage and cheese on the edge of the widest part of the dough.
3. Roll the dough over the sausage and cheese and make a pinch on the seam to seal.
4. Preheat the air fryer to 379°F.
5. Air fry the sausage wraps in batches for 3 minutes.
6. Add the sausage wraps in skewers and serve.

Nutrition- Per Serving: Calories 125kcal, Total Fat:6g, Carbs: 16g, Proteins 5g

Variation: American cheese can be replaced with the desired cheese.

AIR FRYER CINNAMON ROLLS

Preparation Time: 10 minutes
Cooking time: 10 minutes
Serving: 10

Ingredients
- ⅓ cup melted butter
- ⅓ cup brown sugar
- 2 tbsp maple syrup
- ⅓ cup walnuts, chopped
- ¼ cup raisins
- 1 tbsp cinnamon
- 2 tbsp brown sugar
- 1 crescent roll, refrigerated

Directions
1. In a bowl whisk butter, sugar, and maple syrup.
2. Brush an air fryer-safe pan with oil.
3. Pour the sugar mixture into the pan then sprinkle it with walnuts and raisins.
4. In a separate bowl mix the cinnamon and sugar.
5. Cut the crescent roll into 8 pieces without unrolling them.
6. Dip the crescent rolls in the cinnamon mixture then place them in the pan.
7. Air fry the cinnamon rolls at 344°F for 10 minutes flipping them halfway during cooking.
8. Transfer the rolls on a serving platter then spoon the mixture in the pan on top of the rolls.
9. Serve and enjoy.

Nutrition- Per Serving: Calories 143kcal, Total Fat:8g, Carbs: 18g, Proteins 2g

Variations: Walnuts can be replaced with pecans.

AIR FRYER AVOCADO AND EGG PIZZA TOAST

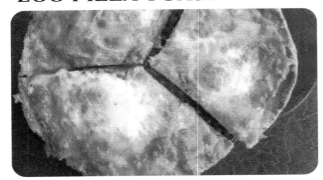

Preparation Time: 10 minutes
Cooking time: 10 minutes
Serving: 4

Ingredients

- 4 bread slices, trimmed
- ¼ cup mayonnaise
- ½ cup cheddar cheese, shredded
- 1 thinly sliced avocado
- 3 eggs
- Salt and black pepper to taste
- ¼ cup mozzarella cheese, shredded

Directions

1. Preheat the air fryer to 399°F and lightly brush the baking pan with cooking spray.
2. Place the bread slices on the pan.
3. Spread ¾ of the mayonnaise on the bread slices then sprinkle them with ¾ of cheddar cheese.
4. Fill the wall and center of the pan with the avocado slices so that the pizza will look like a peace symbol with 3 compartments.
5. Crack each egg onto each of the compartments and spread the remaining mayonnaise over the eggs.
6. Sprinkle the avocado with salt, pepper, and the remaining cheddar cheese.
7. Place the pan in the air fryer and cook for 7 minutes.
8. Sprinkle the mozzarella on the pizza and cook it for an additional 3 minutes.
9. Serve and enjoy.

Nutrition- Per Serving: Calories 302kcal, Total Fat:28g, Carbs: 4g, Proteins 10g
Variation: The desired cheese can be used.

AIR FRYER PANCAKES

Preparation Time: 10 minutes
Cooking time: 10 minutes
Serving: 4

Ingredients

- 1 ½ cup all-purpose flour
- 3 ½ tbsp baking powder
- 1 ½ tbsp baking soda
- 1 tbsp salt
- 1 tbsp sugar
- 1 ¼ cup milk
- 1 egg
- 3 tbsp butter, melted

Directions

1. In a bowl mix all the ingredients until they are well combined.
2. Allow the batter to stand for 4 minutes.
3. Preheat the air fryer to 201°F and spray the air fryer safe pan with cooking spray.
4. Spread the batter on the pan with the desired thickness.
5. Cook each pancake for 3 minutes until all batter is finished.
6. Serve and enjoy.

Nutrition- Per Serving: Calories 346kcal, Total Fat:14g, Carbs: 48g, Proteins 10g

Variation: The butter can be replaced with cooking oil.

AIR FRYER BISCUITS AND GRAVY

Preparation Time: 10 minutes
Cooking time: 15 minutes
Serving: 6
Ingredients
Gravy Ingredients:
- 1 lb ground sausage, browned
- 4 oz cream cheese, melted
- ½ cup water
- ½ cup heavy whipping cream
- ½ tbsp garlic powder
- 1 tbsp xanthan gum
- Salt and black pepper to taste

Biscuit Ingredients:
- 2 cups Carb Quick
- ¼ cup cubed butter
- ½ tbsp garlic powder
- ½ tbsp salt
- ¼ cup heavy whipping cream
- ¼ cup water

Directions
1. Mix all the gravy ingredients in a bowl until well combined.
2. Transfer the gravy to the air fryer-safe pan.
3. In a separate bowl mix the Carb Quick with butter.
4. Stir in the garlic, salt, cream, and water to the Carb Quick mixture until a smooth dough is formed.
5. Make small biscuits from the dough and add them to the gravy.
6. Air fry the biscuits at 349°F for 15 minutes.
7. Serve and enjoy.

Nutrition- Per Serving: Calories 690kcal, Total Fat:60g, Carbs: 40g, Proteins: 29g
Variation: The Carb Quick can be replaced with homemade biscuit dough.

AIR FRYER SCRAMBLED EGGS

Preparation Time: 3 minutes
Cooking time: 7 minutes
Serving: 2

Ingredients
- ⅓ tbsp unsalted butter, melted
- 2 eggs, beaten
- 2 tbsp milk
- Salt and black pepper to taste
- ⅛ cup cheddar cheese

Directions
1. In a bowl whisk the butter, eggs, milk, salt, and pepper.
2. Transfer the mixture to an air fryer-safe pan and cook it for 300°F for 3 minutes.
3. Stir the eggs then cook them for an additional 2 minutes.
4. Stir the cheese into the eggs then cook for 2 minutes.
5. Remove the eggs from the pan and serve.

Nutrition- Per Serving: Calories 126kcal, Total Fat:5g, Carbs: 1g, Proteins: 9g

Variation: The preferred cheese can be used.

SNACK & APPETIZER

AIR FRYER FRENCH FRIES

Preparation Time: 10 minutes
Cooking Time: 15 minutes
Serving: 2

Ingredients
- Cooking spray
- 1 russet potato, unpeeled
- 1 tbsp olive oil
- Salt and black pepper to taste

Directions
1. Preheat the air fryer to 381°F and spray the air fryer basket with cooking spray.
2. Slice the potato lengthwise into ¼ inch sticks.
3. Rinse the potato piece with clean water then dry them using a paper towel.
4. Add the potato pieces to a bowl.
5. Pour oil over the potato pieces then sprinkle them with salt and pepper.
6. Toss the potato sticks until well coated.
7. Transfer the potato sticks to an air fryer basket in a single layer.
8. Cook the fries for 15 minutes turning them halfway during cooking.
9. Serve and enjoy.

Nutrition-Per Serving: Calories: 214Kcal, Total Fat: 7g, Carbs: 35g, Protein: 4g

Variation: The desired seasoning can be used.

MOZZARELLA STICKS

Preparation Time: 0 minutes
Cooking Time: 6minutes
Serving: 2

Ingredients
- 6 mozzarella sticks, frozen

Directions
1. Preheat the air fryer to 381°F.
2. Spread the mozzarella sticks in the air fryer basket in a single layer.
3. Air fry the mozzarella sticks for 6 minutes turning them after 4 minutes of cooking.
4. Allow the sticks to cool for about 5 minutes then serve.

Nutrition-Per Serving: Calories: 271Kcal, Total Fat: 16g, Carbs: 22g, Protein: 12g

Variation: Seasoning can be added according to your preference.

AIR FRYER PICKLES

Preparation Time: 10 minutes
Cooking Time: 16 minutes
Serving: 4
Ingredients

- 4 dill pickles, sliced lengthwise
- ½ cup all-purpose flour
- ½ tbsp paprika
- ¼ tbsp garlic powder
- ¼ tbsp black pepper
- ¼ tbsp cayenne pepper
- 1 tbsp salt
- ½ cup buttermilk
- 1 egg
- 1 cup bread crumbs
- 2 tbsp olive oil
- Cooking spray

Directions

1. Pat dry the pickles with a paper towel.
2. In a bowl mix the flour, paprika, garlic powder, black pepper, cayenne pepper, and ½ tablespoon salt.
3. In a separate bowl mix buttermilk, egg, and ¼ cup of the flour mixture.
4. In a different bowl mix the breadcrumbs, remaining salt, and oil until combined.
5. Coat the pickles with flour mixture then dip in the buttermilk mixture and finally coat with the bread crumbs mixture.
6. Spread the pickles in an air fryer basket in a single layer.
7. Cook the pickles at 399°F for 10 minutes.
8. Spray the pickles with cooking spray and cook them for an additional 6 minutes.
9. Serve and enjoy.

Nutrition-Per Serving: Calories: 223Kcal, Total Fat: 10g, Carbs: 25g, Protein: 6g
Variation: Onion powder can be used instead of cayenne pepper.

AIR FRYER ONION RINGS

Preparation Time: 0 minutes
Cooking Time: 4 minutes
Serving: 2

Ingredients

- 6 oz onion rings, frozen

Directions

1. Preheat the air fryer to 349°F.
2. Place the onion rings in the air fryer basket.
3. Air fry the onions for 4 minutes shaking them halfway during cooking.
4. Transfer the onion rings to the serving platter and serve.

Nutrition-Per Serving: Calories: 303Kcal, Total Fat: 17g, Carbs: 36g, Protein: 4g

Variation: Different spicy variations can be used.

AIR FRYER PIZZA SLIDERS

Preparation Time: 10 minutes
Cooking Time: 12 minutes
Serving: 12

Ingredients
- 1 pack dinner rolls
- 1 cup pizza sauce
- 2 cups mozzarella cheese, shredded
- ¼ red onion, diced
- ½ cup mix colored bell peppers
- 6 black olives, sliced
- Salt and black pepper to taste
- ¼ tbsp dry oregano leaves
- Fresh parsley
-

For Garlic Butter:
- ¼ cup unsalted butter, melted
- 1 tbsp dry parsley flakes
- ½ tbsp dry oregano leaves
- ½ tbsp dry Italian seasoning
- ¼ tbsp salt
- 3 tbsp parmesan cheese
-

Directions
1. Preheat the air fryer to 371°F.
2. Mix all the garlic butter ingredients in a bowl until well combined then set aside.
3. Cut the dinner rolls lengthwise into halves.
4. Place one of the halves of the dinner rolls on a flat surface.
5. Spread butter on the dinner roll then the pizza sauce and finally the ½ of mozzarella cheese.
6. Repeat the process for 11 dinner rolls.
7. Divide the onions, bell peppers, olives, salt, black pepper, oregano, and remaining cheese into all the dinner rolls
8. Cook the dinner rolls for 7 minutes.
9. Spread the butter on the remaining dinner rolls then place them over the cheese.
10. Brush the dinner rolls with garlic butter and cook them for 5 minutes.
11. Brush the dinner rolls with more garlic butter and sprinkle parsley then serve.

Nutrition-Per Serving: Calories: 80Kcal, Total Fat: 4g, Carbs: 5g, Protein: 7g

Variation: Marinara sauce can be used in place of pizza sauce

AIR FRYER PIZZA MARGHERITA

Preparation Time: 5 minutes
Cooking Time: 7 minutes

Ingredients

- Buffalo mozzarella
- Pizza dough1 12-inch dough will make 2 personal sized pizzas
- Olive oil
- Tomato sauce
- Optional toppings to finish: fresh basil, parmesan cheese, pepper flakes

Directions

1. Preheat air fryer to 375°F (190°C). Spray air fryer basket well with oil. Dry the mozzarella from its liquid well. (So as to see that the dough gets wet)
2. Roll out pizza dough to the size of your air fryer basket. Carefully transfer it to the air fryer, then brush lightly with a teaspoon or so of olive oil. Spoon on a light layer of tomato sauce and sprinkle with chunks of buffalo mozzarella.
3. For about 7 minutes until crust is crispy and cheese has melted. Optionally top with basil, grated parmesan, and pepper flakes just before serving.

AIR FRYER RAVIOLI

Preparation Time: 5 minutes
Cooking Time: 6 minutes
Serving: 6

Ingredients

- 12 ravioli, frozen
- ½ cup buttermilk
- ½ cup breadcrumbs
- Cooking spray

Directions

1. Preheat the air fryer to 399°F.
2. Place buttermilk and breadcrumbs in 2 different bowls.
3. Dip each ravioli into buttermilk then coat with breadcrumbs.
4. Arrange the breaded ravioli in the air fryer in a single layer.
5. Air fry the ravioli for 6 minutes spraying them with cooking spray halfway during cooking.
6. Serve while hot.

Nutrition-Per Serving: Calories: 480Kcal, Total Fat: 20g, Carbs: 57g, Protein: 20g

Variation: the buttermilk can be replaced with eggs.

AIR FRYER ZUCCHINI CHIPS

Preparation Time: 10 minutes
Cooking Time: 8 minutes
Serving: 4

Ingredients
- 1 zucchini
- ½ cup breadcrumbs
- ½ tbsp garlic powder
- ¼ tbsp onion powder
- 1 egg
- 3 tbsp all-purpose flour

Directions
1. Slice the zucchini into ¼ inch slices.
2. In a bowl, mix the breadcrumbs, garlic powder, and onion powder.
3. Place the egg and flour in separate bowls.
4. Coat the zucchini in flour then dip into the egg and finally coat them with the breadcrumbs.
5. Air fry the zucchini at 379°F for 8 minutes flipping them halfway during cooking.
6. Serve and enjoy.

Nutrition-Per Serving: Calories: 102Kcal, Total Fat: 2g, Carbs: 15g, Protein: 5g

Variation: different seasons can be used depending on your preference.

AIR FRYER SWEET POTATO FRIES

Preparation Time: 4 minutes
Cooking Time: 20 minutes
Serving: 2

Ingredients
- 16 oz sweet potato
- ½ tbsp salt
- ¼ tbsp black pepper
- ¼ tbsp paprika
- 2 tbsp avocado oil

Directions
1. Preheat the air fryer to 379°F.
2. Wash the sweet potato with clean water then slice them into ¼ inch sticks.
3. Dry the sweet potato with a paper towel.
4. In a bowl toss the sweet potato pieces, salt, pepper, paprika, and oil.
5. Transfer the sweet potato into the air fryer basket and cook them for 20 minutes. Shake the basket halfway during cooking.
6. Serve and enjoy.

Nutrition-Per Serving: Calories: 236Kcal, Total Fat: 5g, Carbs: 45g, Protein: 4g

Variation: Coconut oil spray can be used instead of avocado oil.

AIR FRYER CHICKEN WINGS

Preparation Time: 10 minutes
Cooking Time: 15 minutes
Serving: 2

Ingredients
- 1 ½ lb chicken wings
- 2 tbsp olive oil
- 1 tbsp smoked paprika
- 1 tbsp chili powder
- 1 ½ tbsp ground cumin
- 1 ½ tbsp onion powder
- 1 ½ tbsp garlic powder
- 1 ½ tbsp ground black pepper
- 1 ½ tbsp salt
- 1 tbsp cayenne pepper

Directions
1. Preheat the air fryer to 374°F.
2. Rinse the chicken with clean water then dry it with a paper towel.
3. Pour oil over the chicken wings and rub to coat.
4. In a bowl mix the paprika, chili powder, cumin, onion powder, garlic powder, black pepper, salt, and cayenne pepper until well combined.
5. Add the chicken to the seasoning mixture and toss to coat.
6. Transfer the chicken wings to the air fryer.
7. Cook the chicken wings for 15 minutes flipping them halfway during cooking.
8. Serve while warm.

Nutrition-Per Serving: Calories: 335Kcal, Total Fat: 23g, Carbs: 9g, Protein: 25g

Variation: seasonings can be used depending on your preference.

AIR FRYER CHICKPEAS

Preparation Time: 5 minutes
Cooking Time: 17 minutes
Serving: 3

Ingredients
- 16 oz can Garbanzo beans, drained
- Avocado cooking spray
- Chili lime seasoning

Directions
1. Preheat the air fryer to 389°F.
2. Place the chickpeas in the air fryer and cook them for about 5 minutes.
3. Open the basket and spray the chickpeas with cooking spray and shake to coat.
4. Cook the chickpeas for 10 minutes shaking the basket halfway during cooking.
5. Open the basket and add the seasoning and shake to combine.
6. Cook the chickpeas for another 2 minutes.
7. Serve and enjoy.

Nutrition-Per Serving: Calories: 380Kcal, Total Fat: 27g, Carbs: 3g, Protein: 34g

Variation: ranch seasoning can be used instead of chili lime seasoning.

VEGETABLE & SIDE DISHES

AIR FRYER ROASTED ASPARAGUS AND POTATOES

Preparation Time: 10 minutes
Cooking Time: 5 minutes
Serving: 4

Ingredients

- 4 young potatoes cut into small pieces
- 1 lb asparagus, cut into small pieces
- 2 stalks scallions, chopped
- 4 tbsp olive oil
- 1 tbsp dried dill
- 1 tbsp salt
- ½ tbsp black pepper

Directions

1. Place the potatoes in a saucepan then cover them with water.
2. Bring the potatoes to a simmer until tender.
3. Drain the potatoes then set them aside.
4. In a bowl, toss asparagus, scallions, and 2 tablespoons of olive oil.
5. Transfer the asparagus to an air fryer and cook for 5 minutes at 349°F.
6. In a bowl mix the potatoes, roasted asparagus and scallions, remaining oil, dill, salt, and pepper.
7. Serve and enjoy.

Nutrition-Per Serving: Calories: 449Kcal, Total Fat: 14g, Carbs: 73g, Protein: 12g

Variation: The desired spices can be used.

BUTTERMILK AIR FRIED MUSHROOMS

Preparation Time: 30 minutes
Cooking Time: 15 minutes
Serving: 2

Ingredients

- Cooking spray
- 2 cups oyster mushroom
- 1 cup buttermilk
- 1 tbsp salt
- 1 tbsp black pepper
- 1 tbsp garlic powder
- 1 ½ cups all-purpose flour
- 1 tbsp onion powder
- 1 tbsp smoked paprika
- 1 tbsp cumin
- 1 tbsp olive oil

Directions

1. Preheat the air fryer to 374°F and spray the air fryer safe pan with cooking spray.
2. In a bowl toss the mushroom and buttermilk. Allow the mixture to stand for 15 minutes.
3. In a separate bowl mix the flour, salt, pepper, garlic powder, onion powder, paprika, and cumin until well combined.
4. Coat the mushroom with the flour mixture then dip in the buttermilk and finally coat with the flour mixture.
5. Arrange the mushroom on the pan in a single layer leaving some space between each mushroom.
6. Air fry the mushrooms for 5 minutes.
7. Brush the mushrooms with oil then cook for 10 minutes.
8. Serve and enjoy.

Nutrition-Per Serving: Calories: 356Kcal, Total Fat: 10g, Carbs: 58g, Protein: 12g

Variation: the spices can be adjusted to fit your preference.

AIR FRYER EGGPLANT PARMESAN

Preparation Time: 10 minutes
Cooking Time: 20 minutes
Serving: 6
Ingredients

- ½ cup bread crumbs
- 2 tbsp vegan parmesan, grated
- Onion powder to taste
- Garlic powder to taste
- Black pepper to taste
- Salt to taste
- 1 eggplant, sliced
- ½ cup all-purpose four
- ½ cup almond milk
- Cooking spray

For the Toppings:

- ½ cup marinara sauce
- ½ cup vegan mozzarella, shredded
- ½ cup Vegan parmesan, grated

Directions

1. In a bowl mix the bread crumbs, parmesan, onion powder, garlic powder, black pepper, and salt until well combined.

2. Coat the eggplant slices with flour then dip them into almond milk and finally coat them with the breadcrumbs mixture.

3. Spray the eggplant slices lightly with cooking spray.

4. Air fry the eggplant at 390°F for 15 minutes flipping them halfway during cooking.

5. Spoon some marinara sauce over the eggplants then top with the cheeses.

6. Air fry the eggplant for 5 minutes until all the cheese melts.

7. Serve and enjoy.

Nutrition-Per Serving: Calories: 151Kcal, Total Fat: 3g, Carbs: 23g, Protein: 9g

Variation: Vegan buttermilk can be used instead of almond milk.

AIR FRYER BAKED POTATOES

Preparation Time: 10 minutes
Cooking Time: 45 minutes
Serving: 4

Ingredients

- 4 potatoes
- 2 tsp olive oil
- Salt to taste
- Black pepper to taste
- Garlic powder to taste
- Fresh parsley
- 4 tbsp butter
-

Directions

1. Add the potatoes and olive oil into a bowl and toss to coat.

2. Season the potatoes with salt, black pepper, garlic powder, and fresh parsley.

3. Transfer the potatoes to the air fryer and cook at 399°F for 45 minutes.

4. Cut a slice of the potatoes and force the flesh of the potato up.

5. Place 1 tablespoon of butter over each potato.

6. Serve and enjoy.

Nutrition-Per Serving: Calories: 410Kcal, Total Fat: 14g, Carbs: 66g, Protein: 8g

Variation: Cajun spices can be used for the seasoning.

AIR FRYER STUFFED BABY ARTICHOKES

Preparation Time: 20 minutes
Cooking Time: 15 minutes
Serving: 10

Ingredients

- 2 lb baby artichokes
- 4 cups of water
- ¼ cup lemon juice
- 8 oz cream cheese
- 6 oz spinach, frozen
- 8 garlic cloves, minced
- 2 tbsp olive oil
- ½ tbsp sea salt
- ¼ tbsp black pepper
- ½ cup parmesan cheese, grated

Directions

1. Cut the artichoke stems leaving ¼ inch long.
2. Remove the artichokes outer petals then cut them into halves.
3. In a bowl mix water and lemon juice.
4. Place the artichokes in the lime water with the cut side down then set aside.
5. In a bowl mash the cream cheese, spinach, and garlic.
6. Take the artichokes out of the lime water and dry them with a paper towel.
7. In a bowl toss the artichoke, oil, salt, and pepper until well coated.
8. Spread the spinach mixture over each artichoke then sprinkle them with parmesan.
9. Arrange the artichokes in an air fryer and cook them at 399°F for 15 minutes.
10. Serve and enjoy.

Nutrition-Per Serving: Calories: 176Kcal, Total Fat: 12g, Carbs: 13g, Protein: 7g

Variation: Cream cheese can be used in place of parmesan cheese.

AIR FRYER BUFFALO CAULIFLOWER

Preparation Time: 10 minutes
Cooking Time: 12 minutes
Serving: 3

Ingredients

- 12 ½ lb cauliflower head, cut into florets
- ½ cup cayenne pepper sauce
- 2 tbsp butter, melted
- 2 tbsp vinegar
- ⅛ tbsp garlic powder
- Salad dressing

Directions

1. Preheat the air fryer to 399°F
2. In a bowl mix the cauliflower, cayenne pepper sauce, butter, vinegar, and garlic powder until well combined.
3. Transfer the cauliflower to the air fryer basket and cook for 12 minutes. Shake the basket halfway during the cooking.
4. Serve the cauliflower with salad dressing.

Nutrition-Per Serving: Calories: 228Kcal, Total Fat: 20g, Carbs: 11g, Protein: 4g

Variation: Blue cheese dip can be used instead of salad dressing.

AIR FRYER CARROT FRIES

Preparation Time: 5 minutes
Cooking Time: 20 minutes
Serving: 4

Ingredients

- 4 carrots, peeled and sliced lengthwise
- 1 tbsp cornflour
- 1 tbsp paprika
- ½ tbsp garlic powder
- 1 tbsp olive oil
- Salt to taste

Directions

1. Preheat the air fryer to 389°F.
2. In a bowl mix carrots, cornflour, paprika, garlic powder, and olive oil.
3. Transfer the seasoned carrots to the air fryer basket and spread them in a single layer without overlapping.
4. Cook the carrots for 20 minutes flipping them halfway during cooking.
5. Transfer the carrot fries to a serving platter and sprinkle them with salt.
6. Serve and enjoy.

Nutrition-Per Serving: Calories: 30Kcal, Total Fat: 1g, Carbs: 5g, Protein: 1g

Variation: Corn starch can be used in place of cornflour.

AIR FRYER CAULIFLOWER CHICKPEA TACOS

Preparation Time: 10 minutes
Cooking Time: 20 minutes
Serving: 4

Ingredients

- 4 cups cauliflower florets
- 19 oz can of chickpeas, drained and rinsed
- 2 tbsp olive oil
- 2 tbsp taco seasoning
- 8 corn tortilla
- 2 avocado sliced
- 4 cups cabbage, shredded
- Coconut yogurt

Directions

1. Preheat the air fryer to 389°F.
2. In a bowl toss the cauliflower, chickpeas, olive oil, and taco seasoning.
3. Transfer the cauliflower mixture to the air fryer basket and cook for 20 minutes. Shake the basket occasionally during the cooking.
4. Serve the cauliflower and chickpeas in tacos with avocado slices, cabbage, and coconut yogurt.

Nutrition-Per Serving: Calories: 507Kcal, Total Fat: 15g, Carbs: 76g, Protein: 20g

Variation: Coconut yogurt can be replaced with regular yogurt.

AIR FRYER BRUSSELS SPROUTS

Preparation Time: 10 minutes
Cooking Time: 10 minutes
Serving: 4

Ingredients
- 1 lb brussels sprouts, trimmed
- 2 tbsp olive oil
- ¼ tbsp salt
- ¼ tbsp garlic powder

Directions
1. Add all the ingredients into a bowl and toss to coat.
2. Transfer the Brussels to an air fryer basket and cook them at 369°F for about 8 minutes. Shake the basket halfway during the cooking.
3. Plate the Brussels and serve.

Nutrition-Per Serving: Calories: 110Kcal, Total Fat: 7g, Carbs: 11g, Protein: 4g

Variation: Favorite seasonings can be used.

AIR FRYER KALE AND POTATO NUGGETS

Preparation Time: 10 minutes
Cooking Time: 47 minutes
Serving: 4

Ingredients
- 2 cups potatoes, finely chopped
- 1 tbsp extra virgin oil
- 1 garlic clove, minced
- ⅛ cup almond milk
- ¼ tbsp salt
- ⅛ tbsp black pepper
- 4 cups kale, coarsely chopped
- Vegetable oil spray

Directions
1. Add the potatoes and water to a saucepan then bring them to a boil.
2. Cook the potatoes for 30 minutes until they are tender.
3. Drain the potatoes and set them aside.
4. Pour oil into a skillet and heat it over medium heat.
5. Saute garlic for 3 minutes.
6. Add the potatoes, garlic, almond milk, salt, and pepper to a bowl and mash using a potato masher.
7. BrusselsBrusselsStir in kales to the mashed potatoes.
8. Preheat the air fryer to 389°F and spray the air fryer basket with oil spray.
9. Make 1-inch nuggets with the potato-kale mixture.
10. Air fry the nuggets for 14 minutes shaking the basket after 6 minutes.
11. Serve and enjoy.

Nutrition-Per Serving: Calories: 380Kcal, Total Fat: 27g, Carbs: 3g, Protein: 34g

Variation: canola oil can be used in place of extra virgin oil
Brussels

VEGAN RECIPES

AIR FRYER AVOCADO FRIES

Preparation Time: 5 minutes
Cooking Time: 10 minutes
Serving: 2

Ingredients
- 1 ripe avocado, sliced
- 1 cup bread crumbs
- ½ tbsp salt
- ½ can chickpea aquafaba

Directions
1. Preheat the air fryer 389°F.
2. In a bowl mix the breadcrumbs and salt.
3. Pour the aquafaba into a separate bowl.
4. Dip the avocado slice in the aquafaba then coat with bread crumbs.
5. Carefully, arrange the avocado slices in the air fryer basket in a single layer.
6. Air fry the avocado for 10 minutes.
7. Serve and enjoy.

Nutrition-Per Serving: Calories: 295Kcal, Total Fat: 17g, Carbs: 31g, Protein: 8g

Variation: Seasoned cornmeal can be used instead of breadcrumbs.

AIR FRYER GREEN BEANS

Preparation Time: 10 minutes
Cooking Time: 12 minutes
Serving: 4

Ingredients
- 12 oz fresh green bean beans, trimmed
- 1 tbsp sesame oil
- 1 tbsp soy sauce
- 1 tbsp rice wine vinegar
- 1 garlic clove, minced
- ½ tbsp red pepper flakes

Directions
1. Preheat the air fryer to 399°F.
2. Add all the ingredients to a bowl and toss to mix.
3. Allow the green beans to marinate for about 5 minutes.
4. Transfer the green beans to the air fryer and cook for 12 minutes. Shake the basket halfway during the cooking.
5. Serve and enjoy.

Nutrition-Per Serving: Calories: 60Kcal, Total Fat: 4g, Carbs: 7g, Protein: 2g

Variation: Olive oil can be used instead of sesame oil.

AIR FRYER PEACH PIES

Preparation Time: 30 minutes
Cooking Time: 56 minutes
Serving: 8
Ingredients
- 10 oz fresh peaches, peeled and chopped
- 1 tbsp lemon juice
- 3 tbsp granulated sugar
- 1 tbsp vanilla extract
- ¼ tbsp salt
- 1 tbsp cornstarch
- 1 14 oz package rolled unbaked pie crust
- Cooking spray

Directions
1. In a bowl mix the peaches, lemon juice, sugar, vanilla, and salt.
2. Allow the peach mixture to stand for 15 minutes.
3. Drain the peaches and reserve 1 tablespoon of the marinade.
4. In a separate bowl mix the cornstarch, reserved marinade, and the peaches.
5. Make 4-inch circles from the pie crust.
6. Place a spoonful of the peach mixture on each circle and fold the dough over the filling.
7. Crimp the edges of the dough to seal.
8. Make 3 small cuts on top of the pies then coat them with cooking spray.
9. Repeat the process for all the pies
10. Air fry the pies in batches at 349°F for 14 minutes.
11. Serve and enjoy.

Nutrition-Per Serving: Calories: 314Kcal, Total Fat: 15g, Carbs: 43g, Protein: 3g
Variation: Fresh peaches can be replaced with frozen peaches.

AIR FRYER CHERRY TOMATOES

Preparation Time: 5 minutes
Cooking Time: 5 minutes
Serving: 4

Ingredients
- 1 lb cherry tomatoes
- 2 tbsp olive oil
- 1 tbsp salt
- ½ tbsp black pepper

Directions
1. Add all the ingredients to a bowl and toss to coat.
2. Transfer the tomatoes to an air fryer basket.
3. Air fry the tomatoes for 5 minutes at 301°F.
4. Serve and enjoy.

Nutrition-Per Serving: Calories: 133Kcal, Total Fat: 7g, Carbs: 19g, Protein: 1g

Variation: the desired seasonings can be used.

AIR FRYER BUTTERNUT SQUASH

Preparation Time: 10 minutes
Cooking Time: 20 minutes
Serving: 4

Ingredients

- 4 butternut squash, chopped into cubes
- 2 tbsp extra virgin oil
- 1 tbsp maple syrup
- 1 tbsp dried oregano
- ½ tbsp garlic powder
- ½ tbsp smoked paprika
- ½ tbsp salt
- ¼ ground chipotle chili pepper

Directions

1. Add all the ingredients to a bowl and toss to coat.
2. Arrange the butternut to an air fryer basket in a single layer.
3. Air fry the butternut at 399°F for 20 minutes.
4. Serve while hot.

Nutrition-Per Serving: Calories: 140Kcal, Total Fat: 7g, Carbs: 21g, Protein: 2g

Variation: Seasoning the butternuts may be done following your preference.

SALADS AND FALAFELS

Preparation Time: 20 minutes
Cooking Time: 15 minutes
Serving: 2

Ingredients

- 1 (15 ounce) can chickpeas, drained and rinsed
- 1/2 cup cilantro
- 1/4 cup fresh parsley
- 1/2 small onion
- 3 cloves garlic
- 1 teaspoon cumin
- 1 teaspoon coriander
- 1 teaspoon ground paprika
- 1/4 teaspoon Cayenne pepper, more for spicier flavor
- 1/2 teaspoon salt

For the Salad:

- 2 cups lettuce, chopped
- 1/2 cup cherry tomatoes, halved
- 1 small cucumber, cut into slices
- 1/2 cup red onion, cut into slices
- 1/2 cup pitted black olives, slices
- Vegan Tzatziki Sauce

Directions

1. Line the air fryer basket with parchment paper, spray with cooking spray or brush with cooking oil.
2. Add chickpeas to the food processor with cilantro, parsley, onion, garlic, cumin, coriander, paprika, cayenne pepper, salt, and pulse.
3. The mixture shouldn't be processed until smooth but still grainy but able to stick together.
4. Scoop out tablespoon sizes of falafel mixture and roll in between the palm of your hands into balls.
5. Place in a single layer on the parchment paper-lined air fryer. Spray with cooking spray.
6. Bake at 350 for 15 minutes turning halfway.
7. Repeat until all the mixture is used up.

AIR FRYER CAULIFLOWER BITES

Preparation Time: 2 hrs 5 minutes

Cooking Time: 12 minutes

Serving: 4

Ingredients

- 7 oz cauliflower, minced
- 3 ½ oz sweet potato, grated
- 2 ½ oz carrot, grated
- 3 oz parsnips, chopped
- 2 tbsp garlic puree
- 1 tbsp chives
- 1 tbsp paprika
- 1 tbsp mixed spice
- 2 tbsp oregano
- Salt and black pepper to taste
- ½ cup desiccated coconut
- 1 cup gluten-free oats
- Cooking spray

Directions

1. In a bowl mix cauliflower, sweet potato, carrot, and parsnips until well combined.

2. Stir in garlic, chives, paprika, mixed spice, oregano, salt, and pepper to the vegetable mixture.

3. Make medium-sized balls from the vegetable mixture.

4. Refrigerate the veggie balls for 2 hours.

5. Blend the coconut and oats in a blender then transfer the flour to a bowl.

6. Coat the veggie balls with the flour mixture then place them on an air fryer safe pan.

7. Spritz the veggie balls with cooking spray.

8. Cook the veggies at 399°F for 12 minutes rolling the ball after 10 minutes of cooking.

9. Serve and enjoy.

Nutrition-Per Serving: Calories: 213Kcal, Total Fat: 9g, Carbs: 30g, Protein: 6g

Variation: Favorite vegetables can be used.

AIR FRYER TOFU WITH BROCCOLI AND CARROT

Preparation Time: 10 minutes

Cooking Time: 15 minutes

Serving: 4

Ingredients

For the Tofu:

- 14 oz extra-firm tofu
- 1 tbsp sesame oil
- 1 tbsp soy sauce

For the Stirfry:

- 2 sliced carrots
- 1 broccoli, chopped
- 1 tbsp sesame oil

For the Sauce:

- 2 tbsp orange zest
- ½ cup orange juice
- 3 tbsp rice vinegar
- 2 tbsp soy sauce
- 2 tbsp sugar
- 2 tbsp cornstarch
- ¼ tbsp salt
- 2 minced garlic cloves

Directions

1. Preheat the air fryer to 389°F.

2. Add the tofu, sesame oil, and soy sauce to a bowl and toss to mix.

3. Place the tofu in the air fryer basket and cook for 5 minutes.

4. Meanwhile, in a bowl mix the carrots, broccoli, and oil.

5. Stir in the carrots and broccoli to the air fryer and cook for about 2 minutes.

6. Mix all the sauce ingredients until all cornstarch dissolves.

7. Pour the sauce into the skillet and cook until the sauce thickens.

8. Add the tofu and veggies to the skillet and mix.

9. Plate the tofu stir fry and serve.

Nutrition-Per Serving: Calories: 298Kcal, Total Fat: 13g, Carbs: 32g, Protein: 16g

Variation: preferred vegetables may be used.

AIR FRYER SPICY CAULIFLOWER STIR-FRY

Preparation Time: 5 minutes
Cooking Time: 30 minute
Serving: 4

Ingredients

1 cauliflower, cut into florets
2 tbsp olive oil
¾ cup thinly sliced onion
5 garlic cloves, sliced
1 ½ tbsp tamari
1 tbsp rice vinegar
½ tbsp coconut sugar
1 tbsp sriracha
Salt and pepper to taste
2 scallions

Directions

1. Preheat the air fryer to 350°F.
2. Add the cauliflower and oil to a bowl and toss to coat.
3. Place the cauliflower in the air fryer basket and cook for 10 minutes.
4. Stir in the onions to the cauliflower and cook for 10 minutes.
5. Stir in garlic to the cauliflower and cook for 5 minutes.
6. Meanwhile, mix tamari, rice vinegar, coconut sugar, sriracha, salt, and pepper in a bowl.
7. Stir the sauce mixture into the cauliflower and cook for 5 minutes.
8. Plate the cauliflower and garnish with the scallions.
9. Serve and enjoy.

Nutrition-Per Serving: Calories: 93Kcal, Total Fat: 3g, Carbs: 13g, Protein: 3g
Variation: Favorite hot sauce can be used in place of sriracha.

VEGAN BURGER

Preparation Time: 5 minutes
Cooking Time: 10 minutes
Serving: 4

Ingredients

- 14 oz (400g) white beans rinsed and drained (I used cannellini beans)
- 2/3 cup (65g) oats
- 1/4 cup (15g) fresh cilantro finely chopped
- 1/2 small onion grated or very finely diced
- 1/2 bell pepper, deseeded preferably grated or very finely diced
- juice of 1 lemon
- 3 Tablespoon sriracha sauce or tomato sauce
- 1 1/2 teaspoon Italian seasoning or oregano
- 1 teaspoon ground cumin
- 1/2 teaspoon smoked paprika
- 1/2 teaspoon garlic powder
- sea salt to taste

Directions

1.Mash the beans in a mixing bowl.
2.Add in oats, cilantro, onion, bell pepper, lemon juice, sriracha sauce (or tomato sauce), herbs and spices and mix together.
3.Divide and shape into 4 patties.
4.Preheat Air Fryer to 350F/180C. Place patties in the basket, spray with olive oil or cooking spray and cook for 9-10 minutes flipping halfway through.
5.Create burgers with buns, patties and then desired toppings.

Nutrition

Calories: 182kcal, Carbs: 34g, Protein: 10g, Fat: 1g

FISH & SEAFOOD

AIR FRYER SCALLOPS

Preparation Time: 10 minutes
Cooking Time: 8 minutes
Serving: 2

Ingredients
- ⅓ cup mashed potato flakes
- ⅓ cup bread crumbs, seasoned
- ⅛ tbsp salt
- ⅛ tbsp black pepper
- 6 scallops
- 2 tbsp all-purpose flour
- 1 egg, beaten
- Flavored cooking spray.

Directions
1. Preheat the air fryer to 399°F.
2. In a bowl mix the potato flakes, bread crumbs, salt, and pepper.
3. In a separate bowl toss the scallops with flour.
4. Place the egg on a shallow plate.
5. Dip the scallops in the egg then coat them with the potato mixture.
6. Place the scallops in the air fryer basket and spritz them with cooking spray.
7. Cook the scallops for 8 minutes turning them halfway during the cooking.
8. Serve and enjoy.

Nutrition-Per Serving: Calories: 298Kcal, Total Fat: 5g, Carbs: 32g, Protein: 27g

Variation: Favorite seafood seasoning may be used.

AIR FRYER PRETZEL CRUSTED CATFISH

Preparation Time: 10 minutes
Cooking Time: 12 minutes
Serving: 2

Ingredients
- 4 catfish fillets
- ½ tbsp salt
- ½ tbsp black pepper
- 2 eggs
- ⅓ cup dijon mustard
- 2 tbsp 2% milk
- ½ cup all-purpose flour
- 4 cups honey mustard miniature pretzel, crushed
- Cooking spray

Directions
1. Preheat the air fryer to 324°F.
2. Season the catfish with salt and pepper.
3. In a bowl whisk the eggs, dijon mustard, and milk.
4. Place the flour and pretzels in different bowls.
5. Coat the catfish with flour then dip into the egg mixture and finally coat them with pretzels.
6. Arrange the catfish in the air fryer basket then spray them with cooking spray.
7. Cook the catfish for 12 minutes.
8. Serve and enjoy.

Nutrition-Per Serving: Calories: 466Kcal, Total Fat: 14g, Carbs: 44g, Protein: 34g

Variation: Yogurt can be used in place of 2% milk.

AIR FRYER COCONUT SHRIMP & APRICOT SAUCE

Preparation Time: 25 minutes

Cooking Time: 8 minutes

Serving: 6

Ingredients

- Cooking spray
- 1 lb shrimp, uncooked
- 1 cup sweetened coconut, shredded
- ½ cup bread crumbs
- 4 egg whites
- 3 dashes hot sauce
- ¼ tbsp salt
- ¼ tbsp black pepper
- ½ cup all-purpose flour

For the Sauce:

- 1 cup apricot preserves
- 1 tbsp cider vinegar
- ¼ tbsp red pepper flakes, crushed

Directions

1. Preheat the air fryer to 374°F and grease the air fryer-safe pan with cooking spray.

2. Peel and devein the shrimp.

3. In a bowl mix the coconut and the breadcrumbs.

4. In a separate bowl whisk the eggs, hot sauce, salt, and pepper.

5. Place the flour in a different bowl.

6. Coat the shrimp with flour then dip in the egg and finally coat with the coconut mixture.

7. Arrange the shrimps on the air fryer pan.

8. Cook the shrimp for 8 minutes turning them halfway during the cooking.

9. Meanwhile, prepare a sauce by mixing all the sauce ingredients in a saucepan.

10. Cook the sauce over medium heat stirring occasionally until all the preserves melt.

11. Plate the shrimp and serve with the sauce.

Nutrition-Per Serving: Calories: 410Kcal, Total Fat: 10g, Carbs: 57g, Protein: 24g

Variation: Favorite sauce can be prepared.

AIR FRYER CRAB PATTIES

Preparation Time: 20 minutes

Cooking Time: 10 minutes

Serving: 2

Ingredients

- 1 sweet red pepper, chopped
- 1 celery ribs, chopped
- 3 green onions, chopped
- 2 egg whites
- 3 tbsp reduced-fat mayonnaise
- ¼ tbsp horseradish
- ¼ tbsp salt
- 1 cup bread crumbs
- 1 cups lump crabmeat
- Cooking spray

For the Sauce:

- 1 celery rib, chopped
- ⅓ cup reduced-fat mayonnaise
- 1 green onion, chopped
- 1 tbsp sweet pickle relish
- ½ tbsp horseradish
- ¼ tbsp salt

Directions

1. Preheat the air fryer to 374°F.

2. In a bowl mix the pepper, celery, onions, egg whites, mayonnaise, horseradish, and salt.

3. Stir in the crab meat until well combined.

4. Place the breadcrumbs in a separate bowl.

5. Scoop 2 spoonfuls of the crab mixture and make patties.

6. Coat the patties with the breadcrumbs and place them in the air fryer basket.

7. Spritz the crab patties with cooking spray.

8. Cook the patties for 12 minutes flipping them halfway during the cooking.

9. Meanwhile, make a sauce by processing all the sauce ingredients in a food processor.

10. Serve the patties with sauce

Nutrition-Per Serving: Calories: 49Kcal, Total Fat: 2g, Carbs: 3g, Protein: 3g

Variation: Favorite sauce can be prepared.

AIR FRYER SHRIMP TACOS WITH CABBAGE SLAW

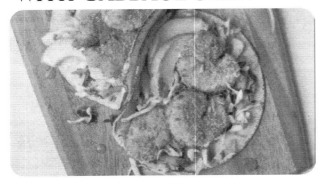

Preparation Time: 5 minutes
Cooking Time: 10 minutes
Serving: 4
Ingredients

- 2 cups coleslaw mix
- ¼ cup fresh cilantro minced
- 2 tbsp lime juice
- 2 tbsp honey
- ¼ tbsp salt
- 1 jalapeno pepper, deceased and minced
- 2 eggs
- ½ cup milk
- ½ cup bread crumbs
- 1 tbsp cumin
- 1 tbsp garlic powder
- ½ cup all-purpose flour
- Cooking spray
- 1 avocado slices

Directions

1. In a bowl add the coleslaw mix, cilantro, lime juice, honey, salt, and jalapeno then toss to coat. Set aside.
2. Preheat the air fryer to 375°F
3. In another bowl whisk the eggs and milk.
4. In a separate bowl mix the breadcrumbs, cumin, and garlic powder.
5. Place the flour in a different bowl.
6. Coat the shrimp with flour then dip in the egg mixture and finally coat them with bread crumbs mixture.
7. Arrange the shrimps in the air fryer basket in a single layer.
8. Spray the shrimps with cooking spray and cook them for 3 minutes.
9. Turn the shrimp and spray them with cooking spray.
10. Cook the shrimp for an additional 3 minutes.
11. Serve the shrimp in tortillas with avocado and coleslaw mix.

Nutrition-Per Serving: Calories: 380Kcal, Total Fat: 27g, Carbs: 3g, Protein: 34g
Variation: cooking spray can be replaced by cooking oil.

AIR FRYER WHOLE SEA BREAM

Preparation Time: 10 minutes
Cooking Time: 16 minutes
Serving: 4

Ingredients

¼ cup all-purpose flour
2 tbsp old bay seasoning
5 garlic cloves, minced
Pinch of salt
1 whole sea bream
Cooking spray

Directions

1. In a bowl mix the flour with old bay seasoning.
2. In a separate bowl mix the garlic and salt.
3. Make several cuts on both sides of the sea bream.
4. Rub the sea bream with the garlic paste then coat it with the seasoned flour.
5. Place the fish in an air fryer tray and spritz with cooking spray.
6. Air fry the fish at 389°F for 16 minutes flipping it halfway through cooking.
7. Serve and enjoy.

Nutrition-Per Serving: Calories: 658Kcal, Total Fat: 23g, Carbs: 8g, Protein: 105g

Variation: Seasoning may be done as desired.

AIR FRYER SPICY BAY SCALLOPS

Preparation Time: 5 minutes
Cooking Time: 10 minutes
Serving: 4

Ingredients

- 1 lb bay scallops, dried
- 2 tbsp smoked paprika
- 2 tbsp chili powder
- 2 tbsp olive oil
- 1 tbsp garlic powder
- ¼ tbsp ground black pepper
- ⅛ tbsp cayenne red pepper

Directions

1. Preheat the air fryer to 399°F.
2. In a bowl mix all the ingredients until well combined.
3. Transfer the scallops to an air fryer basket.
4. Cook the scallops for 8 minutes shaking the basket halfway during the cooking time.
5. Serve and enjoy.

Nutrition-Per Serving: Calories: 380Kcal, Total Fat: 27g, Carbs: 3g, Protein: 34g

Variation: Seasoning of your preference can be used.

OLD BAY GRILLED SHRIMP SKEWERS

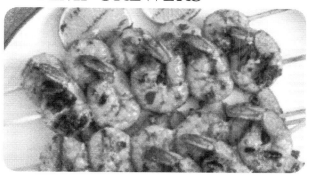

Preparation Time: 10 minutes
Cooking Time: 5 minutes
Serving: 8

Ingredients

- 1 lb shrimp, peeled and deveined
- ½ cup old bay seasoning
- 8 skewers

Directions

1. Thread the shrimp into the skewers
2. Sprinkle the shrimp with the seasoning.
3. Place the skewed shrimp in the air fryer basket.
4. Air fry the shrimp at 399°F for 5 minutes.
5. Serve and enjoy.

Nutrition-Per Serving: Calories: 57Kcal, Total Fat: 1g, Carbs: 0g, Protein: 11g

Variation: Preferred seasoning can be used

AIR FRYER CRUMB-TOPPED SOLE

Preparation Time: 10 minutes
Cooking Time: 10 minutes
Serving: 4

Ingredients
- 3 tbsp mayonnaise
- 3 tbsp parmesan cheese, grated
- 2 tbsp mustard seed
- ¼ tbsp black pepper
- 4 sole fillet
- 1 cup bread crumbs
- 1 finely chopped, green onion
- ½ tbsp ground mustard
- 2 tbsp melted butter
- Cooking spray

Directions
1. Preheat the air fryer to 374°F.
2. In a bowl mix the mayonnaise, 2 tablespoon cheese, mustard seed, and pepper.
3. Spread the mayonnaise mixture on both sides of the fillets.
4. Cook the fillets for 3 minutes.
5. Meanwhile, mix bread crumbs, onion, ground mustard, remaining cheese, and butter in a bowl.
6. Gently spread the bread crumbs mixture on the fillets then mist them with cooking spray.
7. Air fry the fillets for another 3 minutes.
8. Plate the fillets and serve.
Nutrition-Per Serving: Calories: 233Kcal, Total Fat: 10g, Carbs: 8g, Protein: 24g
Variation: Greek yogurt can be used in place of mayonnaise.

SALMON WITH MAPLE-DIJON GLAZE

Preparation Time: 10 minutes
Cooking Time: 6 minutes
Serving: 4

Ingredients
- 3 tbsp butter
- 3 tbsp maple syrup
- 1 tbsp dijon mustard
- 1 lemon juice
- 1 garlic clove, minced
- 4 salmon fillets
- 1 tbsp olive oil
- ¼ tbsp salt
- ¼ tbsp black pepper
-

Directions
1. Preheat the air fryer to 399°F.
2. Melt butter in a saucepan over medium heat.
3. Stir in maple syrup, dijon mustard, lemon juice, and garlic to the butter.
4. Allow the butter mixture to simmer for 3 minutes until the mixture thickens. Remove from heat and set aside.
5. Brush the salmon with oil and season it with salt and pepper.
6. Place the salmon in the air fryer basket and cook for 6 minutes.
7. Serve the fillet with the prepared sauce.

Nutrition-Per Serving: Calories: 329Kcal, Total Fat: 24g, Carbs: 11g, Protein: 20g
Variation: Dijon mustard can be replaced with soy sauce.

AIR FRYER POULTRY RECIPES

AIR FRYER CHICKEN T ENDERS

Preparation Time: 5 minutes
Cooking Time: 30 minutes
Serving: 4

Ingredients
- 1 ¼ lb chicken tenders
- 2 eggs, beaten
- 1 tbsp salt
- Black pepper to taste
- ½ cup seasoned breadcrumbs
- Olive oil spray
- Lemon wedges

Directions
1. Season the chicken with salt and pepper.
2. Place the egg and breadcrumbs in separate bowls.
3. Dip the chicken in the egg then coat it with breadcrumbs.
4. Spritz the chicken tenders with olive oil spray.
5. Preheat the air fryer to 399°F.
6. Cook the chicken in batches for 6 minutes on each side.
7. Serve the chicken tenders with lemon wedges.

Nutrition-Per Serving: Calories: 291Kcal, Total Fat: 7g, Carbs: 17g, Protein: 39g

Variation: Almond flour can be used in place of breadcrumbs.

AIR FRYER CHICKEN DRUMSTICKS

Preparation Time: 5 minutes
Cooking Time: 20 minutes
Serving: 4

Ingredients
- 1 tbsp sea salt
- 1 tbsp fresh cracked pepper
- 1 tbsp garlic powder
- 1 tbsp paprika
- ½ tbsp cumin
- 8 chicken drumsticks
- 2 tbsp olive oil

Directions
1. In a bowl mix salt, pepper, garlic powder, paprika, and cumin.
2. Add the chicken and oil to a separate bowl and toss to coat.
3. Sprinkle the seasoning over the chicken.
4. Preheat the air fryer to 399°F.
5. Transfer the drumsticks to an air fryer basket.
6. Cook the drumsticks for 20 minutes flipping them halfway through cooking.
7. Serve while hot.

Nutrition-Per Serving: Calories: 200Kcal, Total Fat: 12g, Carbs: 1g, Protein: 23g

Variation: Favorite seasonings can be used.

AIR FRYER CHICKEN AND BROCCOLI

Preparation Time: 10 minutes
Cooking Time: 20 minutes
Serving: 4
Ingredients

- 3 tbsp olive oil
- ½ tbsp garlic powder
- 1 tbsp minced ginger
- 1 tbsp low sodium soy sauce
- 1 tbsp rice vinegar
- 1 tbsp sesame oil
- 2 tbsp hot sauce
- ½ tbsp salt
- Black pepper to taste
- 1 lb chicken breast, boneless
- and skinless
- ½ lb broccoli florets
- ½ lb onion, sliced

Directions

1. Preheat the air fryer to 379°F
2. Make the marinade by mixing olive oil, garlic powder, ginger, soy sauce, vinegar, sesame oil, hot sauce, salt, and pepper.
3. Place the chicken in a bowl and pour half of the marinade. Stir to coat.
4. In a separate bowl, mix the broccoli, onions, and remaining marinade.
5. Allow the chicken and the broccoli to stand for 5 minutes.
6. Transfer the chicken to an air fryer tray and cook for 10 minutes.
7. Add the broccoli and the marinade to the air fryer.
8. Cook the chicken and broccoli for 10 minutes stirring them halfway during cooking.
9. Serve while warm.

Nutrition-Per Serving: Calories: 224Kcal, Total Fat: 10g, Carbs: 3g, Protein: 26g
Variation: Apple cider vinegar can be used in place of rice vinegar.

AIR FRYER TURKEY BREAST

Preparation Time: 5 minutes
Cooking Time: 55 minutes
Serving: 10

Ingredients

- 4 lb turkey breast, skin in
- 1 tbsp olive oil
- 2 tbsp salt
- ½ tbsp dry turkey seasoning

Directions

1. Rub the turkey with oil.
2. Season the turkey with salt and dry turkey seasoning.
3. Preheat the air fryer to 349°F.
4. Place the turkey in the air fryer basket with the skin side down.
5. Cook the turkey for 20 minutes.
6. Turn the turkey and cook for an additional 35 minutes.
7. Allow the turkey to cool for 10 minutes then serve.

Nutrition-Per Serving: Calories: 226Kcal, Total Fat: 10g, Carbs: 0g, Protein: 33g

Variation: Poultry seasoning can be used in place of dry turkey seasoning.

AIR FRYER TURKEY CUTLETS

Preparation Time: 10 minutes
Cooking Time: 10 minutes
Serving: 2

Ingredients
- 2 turkey cutlets
- 1 tbsp butter
- Salt and black pepper to taste
- Parsley

For the Mushroom Sauce:
- 1 can of cream of mushroom soup
- ½ cup milk
- Pinch of pepper

Directions
1. Preheat the air fryer to 379°F.
2. Spread the butter on the turkey cutlets then sprinkle them with salt and pepper.
3. Place the turkey cutlets in an air fryer basket and cook for 10 minutes.
4. Meanwhile, prepare the mushroom sauce by mixing the sauce ingredients in a saucepan.
5. Cook the sauce over medium heat for 8 minutes stirring occasionally.
6. Plate the turkey cutlets.
7. Serve cutlets with mushroom sauce and sprinkled parsley.

Nutrition-Per Serving: Calories: 380Kcal, Total Fat: 27g, Carbs: 3g, Protein: 34g

Variation: Mushroom sauce can be swapped out with favorite gravy

CHEDDAR RANCH CHICKEN TENDERS

Preparation Time: 10 minutes
Cooking Time: 25 minutes
Serving: 8

Ingredients
- Cooking spray
- 2 tbsp all-purpose flour
- 2 tbsp Montreal chicken seasoning
- ⅔ bread crumbs
- ½ cup sharp cheddar cheese
- ⅓ cup ranch dressing
- 14 oz chicken tenders, boneless and skinless

Directions
1. Line the air fryer basket with parchment paper then spray it with cooking spray.
2. In a bowl, mix the flour and chicken seasoning.
3. In another bowl mix the bread crumbs and cheese.
4. Place the ranch dressing in a different bowl.
5. Coat the chicken with flour mixture, dip it into ranch dressing, and finally coat them with the bread crumb mixture.
6. Preheat the air fryer to 324°F.
7. Transfer the chicken to the air fryer basket and cook for 10 minutes.
8. Turn the chicken then cook for an additional 15 minutes.
9. Serve and enjoy.

Nutrition-Per Serving: Calories: 150Kcal, Total Fat: 7g, Carbs: 8g, Protein: 13g

Variation: Ranch dressing can be replaced with mayonnaise.

AIR FRYER PARMESAN CRUSTED CHICKEN

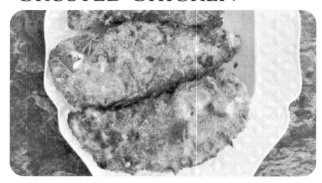

Preparation Time: 5 minutes
Cooking Time: 15 minutes
Serving: 4

Ingredients
- 2 chicken breast
- 1 cup shredded parmesan
- 1 cup bread crumbs
- 1 cup mayonnaise
- 1 tbsp garlic powder
- Parsley for garnishing

Directions
1. Cut the chicken breast into halves and pound it with a meat hammer.
2. Sprinkle the chicken with salt.
3. Spread the mayonnaise on both sides of the chicken breasts.
4. In a bowl mix the bread crumbs, parmesan, and garlic powder.
5. Coat the chicken with the bread crumbs mixture then transfer them to the air fryer basket.
6. Air fry the chicken at 389°F for 15 minutes turning them after 10 minutes.
7. Sprinkle some parsley and serve.

Nutrition-Per Serving: Calories: 663Kcal, Total Fat: 50g, Carbs: 20g, Protein: 31g
Variation: Bread crumbs can be swapped out with an almond meal.

AIR FRYER CHICKEN KEBAB

Preparation Time: 1 hr
Cooking Time: 15 minutes
Serving: 4

Ingredients
- ¼ cup full-fat greek yogurt
- 1 tbsp minced garlic
- 1 tbsp tomato paste
- 1 tbsp vegetable oil
- 1 tbsp lemon juice
- 1 tbsp salt
- 1 tbsp ground cumin
- 1 tbsp smoked paprika
- ½ tbsp ground cinnamon
- ½ tbsp black pepper
- ½ tbsp cayenne pepper
- 1 lb chicken thighs, boneless and skinless
- 4 skewers

Directions
1. In a bowl mix all the ingredients except the chicken until they are well combined.
2. Cut the chicken into 1-inch pieces.
3. Add the chicken pieces to the marinade and mix.
4. Let the chicken marinate for 30 minutes.
5. Place the chicken in the air fryer basket.
6. Set the air fryer to preheat at 369°F.
7. Cook the chicken for 15 minutes flipping them after 10 minutes.
8. Add the chicken pieces onto the skewers.
9. Serve and enjoy.

Nutrition-Per Serving: Calories: 298Kcal, Total Fat: 23g, Carbs: 3g, Protein: 20g
Variation: Sour cream can be used in place of greek yogurt.

AIR FRYER CHICKEN NUGGETS

Preparation Time: 15 minutes
Cooking Time: 8 minutes
Serving: 4

Ingredients
- 1 lb chicken tender, cut into 2-inch pieces
- 1 package dry ranch salad dressing mix
- 2 tbsp flour
- 1 egg, beaten
- 1 cup bread crumbs
- Olive oil cooking spray
- Parsley for garnishing

Directions
1. Add the chicken and ranch seasoning to a bowl then toss to coat. Allow the chicken to stand for 10 minutes.
2. Place flour, egg, and bread crumbs in different shallow plates.
3. Coat the chicken pieces with flour then dip in the egg and finally coat them with bread crumbs.
4. Preheat the air fryer to 389°F and grease the air fryer basket with cooking spray.
5. Arrange the chicken pieces in the air fryer basket without overlapping.
6. Spritz the chicken nuggets with cooking spray.
7. Air fry the nuggets for 8 minutes turning them halfway through cooking.
8. Garnish the nuggets with parsley and serve while hot.

Nutrition-Per Serving: Calories: 244Kcal, Total Fat: 4g, Carbs: 25g, Protein: 31g
Variation: Melted butter can be used in place of the egg.

AIR FRYER TURKEY CROQUETTES

Preparation Time: 20 minutes
Cooking Time: 10 minutes
Serving: 6

Ingredients
- 2 cups potatoes, mashed
- ½ cup parmesan cheese, grated
- ½ cup swiss cheese, shredded
- 1 finely chopped shallot
- 2 tbsp fresh rosemary, minced
- 1 tbsp fresh sage, minced
- ½ tbsp salt
- ¼ tbsp pepper
- 3 cups cooked turkey, chopped
- 1 egg
- 2 tbsp water
- 1 cup bread crumbs
- Butter flavored cooking spray
- Sour cream

Directions
1. Preheat the air fryer to 349°F.
2. In a bowl mix the potatoes, cheeses, shallot, rosemary, sage, salt, and pepper.
3. Stir in the turkey to the potato mixture.
4. Make 1-inch patties from the turkey mixture.
5. In a separate bowl whisk the egg and water.
6. Place the bread crumbs in a different bowl.
7. Dip the croquettes in the egg mixture then coat them with the bread crumbs.
8. Place the croquettes in the air fryer in a single layer and mist them with cooking spray.
9. Cook the croquettes for 10 minutes flipping them halfway through cooking.
10. Serve with sour cream.

Nutrition-Per Serving: Calories: 322Kcal, Total Fat: 12g, Carbs: 21g, Protein: 29g
Variation: Dried sage leaves can be used instead of fresh sage.

AIR FRYER SESAME CHICKEN THIGHS

Preparation Time: 5 minutes
Cooking Time: 15 minutes
Serving: 4

Ingredients

- 2 tbsp sesame oil
- 2 tbsp soy sauce
- 1 tbsp honey
- 1 tbsp sriracha sauce
- 1 tbsp rice vinegar
- 2 lb chicken thighs
- 1 chopped green onion
- 2 tbsp sesame seeds, toasted

Directions

1. In a bowl mix sesame oil, Soy sauce, honey, sriracha, and vinegar.
2. Stir the chicken into the marinade and refrigerate for 30 minutes.
3. Preheat the air fryer to 399°F.
4. Drain the marinade and transfer the chicken to an air fryer basket.
5. Cook the chicken thigh for 15 minutes flipping them after 5 minutes.
6. Plate the chicken thighs and garnish with green onion and sesame seeds.
7. Serve and enjoy.

Nutrition-Per Serving: Calories: 485Kcal, Total Fat: 33g, Carbs: 7g, Protein: 40g

Variation: Sesame oil can be replaced with olive oil.

BACON WRAPPED STUFFED CHICKEN

Preparation Time: 15 minutes
Cooking Time: 30minutes
Serving: 4

Ingredients

- 2 chicken breasts
- ½ cup spinach
- ¼ cup cream cheese
- ¼ cup parmesan cheese, shredded
- 2 tbsp chopped jalapeno peppers
- 1 tbsp black pepper
- ½ tbsp salt
- 6 bacon slices
- 4 tbsp cajun seasoning

Directions

1. Cut the chicken breast into halves then pound them into ½ -inch thickness.
2. In a bowl mix the spinach, cream cheese, parmesan, jalapeno, pepper, and salt.
3. Spread the spinach mixture over the chicken breasts.
4. Roll the chicken breast so that the filling remains inside.
5. Rub the chicken with cajun seasoning.
6. Wrap each chicken with 3 bacon slices then place in an air fryer basket.
7. Set the chicken to air fry at 350°F for 30 minutes.
8. Serve and enjoy.

Nutrition-Per Serving: Calories: 357Kcal, Total Fat: 24g, Carbs: 3g, Protein: 34g
Variation: De-boned chicken thighs can be used in place of chicken breast.

AIR FRYER TURKEY STUFFED PEPPERS

Preparation Time: 15 minutes
Cooking Time: 15 minutes
Serving: 3
Ingredients

- Cooking spray
- 3 red bell pepper
- 1 tbsp olive oil
- 12 oz ground turkey
- ½ cup brown rice, cooked
- ¼ cup bread crumbs
- ¾ cup low-sodium marinara sauce
- 3 tbsp finely chopped parsley
- ¼ tbsp ground pepper
- ¼ cup parmesan cheese, grated
- ¼ cup part-skim mozzarella cheese, shredded
- Parsley for garnishing

Directions

1. Preheat the air fryer to 349°F and spray the air fryer basket with cooking spray.
2. Cut off the pepper tops and reserve them. Deseed the peppers then set them aside.
3. Heat oil in a skillet over medium heat.
4. Brown the turkey in the skillet for about 4 minutes.
5. Stir in rice and bread crumbs to the turkey and cook for 1 minute. Remove the turkey from heat.
6. Stir in the marinara, parsley, pepper, and parmesan to the turkey mixture.
7. Divide the turkey mixture among the bell pepper.
8. Cover the bell pepper with reserved pepper tops and place them in the air fryer basket.
9. Cook the stuffed peppers for 8 minutes.
10. Remove the pepper tops and sprinkle mozzarella over the peppers.
11. Cook the stuffed peppers for 2 minutes.
12. Sprinkle the peppers with parsley and serve.

Nutrition-Per Serving: Calories: 407Kcal, Total Fat: 21g, Carbs: 26g, Protein: 29g

Variation: Green peppers can be used instead of red bell peppers.

AIR FRYER BUFFALO CHICKEN CASSEROLE

Preparation Time: 10 minutes
Cooking Time: 15 minutes
Serving: 4
Ingredients

- 4 cups rotisserie chicken, shredded
- ½ cup chopped onion
- ¼ cup cream
- ¼ cup hot wing sauce
- ¼ cup blue cheese, crumbled
- 2 oz cream cheese, diced
- Salt and black pepper to taste
- ¼ cup green scallions, chopped

Directions

1. Preheat the air fryer to 349°F and coat a baking dish with cooking spray.
2. Mix all the ingredients in a bowl until they are well combined.
3. Transfer the chicken mixture to the baking dish.
4. Place the baking dish in an air fryer and cook for 15 minutes.
5. Remove the dish from the air fryer and cover with a foil for 3 minutes.
6. Garnish the chicken casserole with green onions then serve.

Nutrition-Per Serving: Calories: 348Kcal, Total Fat: 22g, Carbs: 3g, Protein: 34g

Variation: Hot wing sauce can be replaced with sriracha sauce.

BEEF, PORK, AND LAMB RECIPES

AIR FRYER HERBED LAMB CHOPS

Preparation Time: 1 hr 5 minutes
Cooking Time: 7 minutes
Serving: 4

Ingredients
- 1 tbsp rosemary
- 1 tbsp thyme
- 1 tbsp oregano
- 1 tbsp salt
- 1 tbsp coriander
- 2 tbsp olive oil
- 2 tbsp lemon juice
- 1 lb lamb chops

Directions
1. Add all the ingredients except the lamb in a resealable bag and shake to mix.
2. Add the lamb chops in the bag and shake to coat then refrigerate for 1 hour.
3. Preheat the air fryer to 389°F.
4. Place the lamb chops in the air fryer and cook for 7 minutes. Flip the lamb chops after 3 minutes of cooking.
5. Plate the lamb chops and serve.

Nutrition-Per Serving: Calories: 414Kcal, Total Fat: 37g, Carbs: 1g, Protein: 19g

Variation: Favorite seasoning can be used.

AIR FRYER LAMB MEATBALLS

Preparation Time: 5 minutes
Cooking Time: 12 minutes
Serving: 4

Ingredients
- 1 lb ground lamb
- 1 tbsp ground cumin
- 2 tbsp granulated onion
- 2 tbsp fresh parsley
- ¼ tbsp ground cinnamon
- Salt and black pepper
- Cooking spray
-

Directions
1. In a bowl thoroughly mix the lamb, cumin, onion, parsley, cinnamon, salt, and black pepper until well combined.
2. Make 1-inch balls from the lamb mixture.
3. Lightly mist the meatballs with cooking spray then place them in an air fryer basket.
4. Air fry the meatballs at 349°F for 15 minutes shaking the basket halfway through cooking.
5. Serve and enjoy.

Nutrition-Per Serving: Calories: 328Kcal, Total Fat: 22g, Carbs: 1g, Protein: 27g

Variation: Dried parsley can be used instead of fresh parsley

PARMESAN AIR FRYER PORK CHOPS

Preparation Time: 5 minutes
Cooking Time: 10 minutes
Serving: 4

Ingredients
- ½ cup grated parmesan
- 1 tbsp salt
- 1 tbsp smoked paprika
- ½ tbsp dried mustard powder
- ½ tbsp garlic powder
- ½ tbsp ground black pepper
- 4 pork chops, boneless
- 1 tbsp avocado oil
- Parsley

Directions
1. Preheat the air fryer to 374°F.
2. In a bowl mix the parmesan, salt, paprika, mustard powder, garlic powder, and pepper.
3. Rub the pork chops with oil then coat with the parmesan mixture.
4. Transfer the pork to an air fryer basket.
5. Cook the pork chops for 10 minutes flipping them halfway through cooking.
6. Allow the pork chops to cool for 5 minutes.
7. Serve the pork chops with parsley.

Nutrition-Per Serving: Calories: 310Kcal, Total Fat: 13g, Carbs: 3g, Protein: 41g

Variation: Favorite cheese may be used.

AIR FRYER PORK CHOPS AND BROCCOLI

Preparation Time: 5 minutes
Cooking Time: 10 minutes
Serving: 2

Ingredients
- 2 tbsp avocado oil
- ½ tbsp paprika
- ½ tbsp onion powder
- ½ tbsp garlic powder
- 2 minced garlic cloves
- 1 tbsp salt
- 2 cups broccoli florets
- 2 ½ oz pork chops, bone-in
- 2 tbsp flavored butter

Directions
1. Preheat the air fryer to 349°F.
2. In a bowl mix the oil, paprika, onion powder, garlic powder, garlic cloves, and salt.
3. Rub the pork chops with the seasoning mixture.
4. Transfer the pork chops to an air fryer basket and cook for 5 minutes.
5. Flip the pork chops and add the broccoli.
6. Cook the pork chops and broccoli for 5 minutes stirring them after 3 minutes.
7. Serve the pork chops while hot with a dollop of butter.

Nutrition-Per Serving: Calories: 483Kcal, Total Fat: 30g, Carbs: 12g, Protein: 41g

Variation: zucchini can be used instead of broccoli.

AIR FRYER BEEF STEAK AND MUSHROOM

Preparation Time: 10 minutes
Cooking Time: 15 minutes
Serving: 4

Ingredients
- 1 lb steak, cubed
- 8 oz mushrooms
- 2 tbsp melted butter
- 1 tbsp Worcestershire sauce
- ½ tbsp garlic powder
- Salt and black pepper to taste
- Minced parsley

Directions
1. In a bowl mix all the ingredients until they are well combined.
2. Preheat the air fryer to 399°F.
3. Add the steak and mushroom to an air fryer basket.
4. Cook the steak for 15 minutes shaking the basket 3 times during the cooking.
5. Garnish the steak and mushroom with parsley and serve.

Nutrition-Per Serving: Calories: 609Kcal, Total Fat: 35g, Carbs: 9g, Protein: 68g

Variation: the mushroom can be replaced with a vegetable of your preference.

AIR FRYER BEEF STEAK WRAPPED ASPARAGUS

Preparation Time: 10 minutes
Cooking Time: 10 minutes
Serving: 6

Ingredients
- 4 tbsp balsamic vinegar
- 4 tbsp olive oil
- 1 garlic clove, crushed
- 1 tbsp salt
- 1 lb asparagus, trimmed
- 1 ½ lb beef flank steak, thinly sliced
- 2 cups grape tomatoes, halved
- Olive oil cooking spray

Directions
1. In a bowl mix the vinegar, oil, garlic, and salt.
2. Place 3 asparagus on 1 slice of steak and roll it up.
3. Repeat the process for all the asparagus.
4. Place the wrapped asparagus and tomatoes in the air fryer basket.
5. Brush the wrapped asparagus and tomatoes with the vinegar mixture and cooking spray.
6. Preheat the air fryer to 389°F.
7. Cook the steak for 1o minutes.
8. Serve and enjoy.

Nutrition-Per Serving: Calories: 432Kcal, Total Fat: 29g, Carbs: 6g, Protein: 34g

Variation: Balsamic vinegar can be replaced with apple cider vinegar.

PECAN CRUSTED AIR FRYER PORK CHOPS

Preparation Time: 10 minutes
Cooking Time: 12 minutes
Serving: 6

Ingredients
- 1 cup pecan pieces
- ⅓ cup arrowroot
- 2 tbsp Italian seasoning
- 1 tbsp onion powder
- 1 tbsp garlic powder
- ¼ tbsp salt
- 1 egg
- 1 tbsp dijon mustard
- 1 tbsp water
- 2 garlic cloves
- 6 pork chops, boneless and trimmed off the fat
- Parsley for garnishing

Directions
1. Preheat the air fryer to 399°F.
2. In a bowl mix the pecan, arrowroot, Italian seasoning, onion powder, garlic powder, salt, egg, Dijon, water, and garlic.
3. Coat both sides of the pork chops with the pecan mixture and transfer them to an air fryer basket.
4. Cook the pork for 12 minutes flipping them after 7 minutes.
5. Garnish the pork chops with parsley and serve.

Nutrition-Per Serving: Calories: 361Kcal, Total Fat: 16g, Carbs: 8g, Protein: 43g

Variation: Arrowroot can be replaced with corn starch.

AIR FRYER ROAST LAMB RACK WITH LEMON CRUST

Preparation Time: 15 minutes
Cooking Time: 30 minutes
Serving: 4

Ingredients
- 1 ¾ lb rack of lamb
- Salt and black pepper to taste
- ½ cup breadcrumbs
- 1 tbsp garlic clove, grated
- 1 tbsp cumin seeds
- 1 tbsp ground cumin
- 1 tbsp oil
- ¼ lemon rinds, grated
- 1 egg, beaten

Directions
1. Preheat the air fryer to 212°F.
2. Season the rack of lamb with salt and pepper then set aside.
3. In a bowl mix the bread crumbs, garlic, cumin seeds, ground cumin, oil, and lemon rinds.
4. Place the egg on a shallow plate.
5. Dip the rack of lamb in the egg then coat with the bread crumbs mixture.
6. Place the lamb in the air fryer basket and cook for 25 minutes.
7. Raise the air fryer temperature to 392°F and cook the lamb for an additional 5 minutes.
8. Allow the lamb to stand for 10 minutes then serve.

Nutrition-Per Serving: Calories: 400Kcal, Total Fat: 24g, Carbs: 4g, Protein: 44g
Variation: Bread crumbs can be replaced with oatmeal.

MINT LAMB WITH TOASTED HAZELNUTS AND PEAS

Preparation Time: 5 minutes
Cooking Time: 35 minutes
Serving: 4

Ingredients
- 2 oz hazelnuts
- 20 oz shoulder of lamb
- 1 tbsp hazelnut oil
- Salt and black pepper to taste
- 2 tbsp freshly chopped mint leaves
- 2 oz frozen peas
- ⅓ cup water
- ½ cup white wine vinegar
- Mint leaves for topping

Directions
1. Air fry the hazelnuts at 320°F for 10 minutes.
2. In a bowl mix the lamb, hazelnut oil, salt, and pepper.
3. Add the mint on one side of the air fryer followed by the lamb then the hazelnuts on top.
4. Add peas on the other side of the air fryer.
5. Pour water and vinegar over the hazelnuts and peas and air fry at 320°F for 25 minutes.
6. Plate the lamb hazelnuts and peas then top with mint.
7. Serve and enjoy.

Nutrition-Per Serving: Calories: 380Kcal, Total Fat: 27g, Carbs: 3g, Protein: 34g

Variation: White wine vinegar can be replaced with apple cider vinegar.

AIR FRYER PORK AND PINEAPPLE

Preparation Time: 5 minutes
Cooking Time: 10 minutes
Serving: 4

Ingredients
- 2 boneless pork chops, cut into 2-inch chunks
- 1 pineapple, peeled and cut into 2-inch chunks
- 1 tbsp fresh parsley, chopped
- 4 skewers

Directions
1. Thread the skewers by alternating the pork chops and pineapple.
2. Preheat the air fryer to 349°F.
3. Cook the kabobs for 10 minutes.
4. Sprinkle the kabobs with parsley and serve.

Nutrition-Per Serving: Calories: 155Kcal, Total Fat: 3g, Carbs: 10g, Protein: 21g

Variation: Additional seasoning may be used if desired.

DESSERT RECIPES

AIR FRYER UBE GLAZED DONUTS

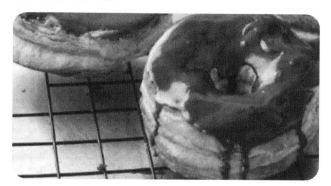

Preparation Time: 5 minutes
Cooking Time: 6 minutes
Serving: 8

Ingredients
- 1 cup powdered sugar
- 2 tbsp 2% milk
- ½ tbsp Ube extract
- ½ tbsp vanilla extract
- 16 oz flaky layers Biscuits

Directions
1. Preheat the air fryer to 349°F and spray the air fryer basket with cooking spray.
2. In a bowl mix powdered sugar, milk, Ube extract, vanilla extract until well combined.
3. Place the biscuits on a flat surface and make holes at the center using a 1-inch cookie cutter.
4. Place the donuts in the air fryer and cook them for 6 minutes. Flip the donut after 3 minutes.
5. Place the donuts on a cooling rack and drizzle Ube glaze over.
6. Allow the donuts to cool then serve.

Nutrition-Per Serving: Calories: 236Kcal, Total Fat: 7g, Carbs: 27g, Protein: 3g

Variation: 2% milk can be replaced with almond milk.

AIR FRIED OREO

Preparation Time: 5 minutes
Cooking Time: 5 minutes
Serving: 8

Ingredients
- 1 package of Pillsbury crescent rolls
- 8 oreo cookies
- Powdered sugar

Directions
1. Spread the crescent roll on a flat surface.
2. Cut the dough into 8 pieces.
3. Place an oreo cookie at the center of the dough.
4. Stretch and fold the corners of the crescent dough to cover the oreo cookie.
5. Preheat the air fryer to 319°F.
6. Place the Oreos in the air fryer basket and cook them for 5 minutes.
7. Remove the Oreos from the air fryer and dust them with powdered sugar.
8. Let the Oreos cool then serve.

Nutrition-Per Serving: Calories: 172Kcal, Total Fat: 4g, Carbs: 32g, Protein: 3g

Variation: Crescent dough sheets can be used instead of Pillsbury crescent roll.

AIR FRYER CHEESECAKE

Preparation Time: 15 minutes
Cooking Time: 34 minutes
Serving: 12

Ingredients

- 30z biscuits
- 2 ½ oz melted butter
- 14 oz caster sugar
- 26 oz feta cheese
- 3 eggs, beaten
- ¼ cups Greek yogurt
- 1 tbsp vanilla essence
- Cheesecake crust

Directions

1. Pulse the biscuits in a blender until fine crumbs are formed.
2. Mix the butter and biscuit crumbs in a bowl.
3. Add the sugar and cheese to a bowl then mix with a hand mixer until the mixture gets fluffy.
4. Add the eggs, Greek yogurt, vanilla, and butter mixture to the cheese mixture. Mix using the hand mixer.
5. Transfer the cheesecake filling to a cheesecake crust.
6. Air fry the cheesecake at 321°F for 30 minutes.
7. Allow the cake to cool for 30 minutes in the air fryer.
8. Cool the cheesecake in the refrigerator for additional 6 hours.
9. Serve and enjoy.

Nutrition-Per Serving: Calories: 447Kcal, Total Fat: 28g, Carbs: 39g, Protein: 6g
Variation: feta cheese can be replaced with any favorite soft cheese.

AIR FRYER CHOCOLATE CUPCAKES

Preparation Time: 10 minutes
Cooking Time: 12 minutes
Serving: 12

Ingredients

- Cooking spray
- ½ cup unsweetened cocoa powder
- ½ cup hot water
- 1 cup sugar
- ¼ cup vegetable oil
- ½ cup milk
- 1 egg, beaten
- 1 tbsp vanilla extract
- 1 cup flour
- ¾ tbsp baking powder
- ¾ tbsp baking soda
- ½ tbsp salt

For the Chocolate Buttercream:

- 8 tbsp softened butter
- 2 cups powdered sugar
- 3 tbsp cocoa powder
- Pinch of salt
- ¼ tbsp vanilla extract
- 4 tbsp milk

Directions

1. Preheat the air fryer to 310°F and spray the silicone cupcakes holders with cooking spray.
2. In a bowl whisk cocoa and water until the powder is dissolved completely.
3. Stir in the sugar, oil, milk, egg, and vanilla extract to the cocoa water.
4. Sift flour, baking powder, baking soda, and salt over the cocoa mixture then mix until well combined.
5. Pour the batter into the cupcake holders and transfer them to an air fryer basket.
6. Cook the cupcakes for 12 minutes.
7. Transfer the cupcakes to a cooling rack and allow them to cool completely.
8. Meanwhile add the butter, sugar, cocoa powder, salt, and vanilla extract to a bowl and mix using a hand mixer.
9. Gradually add milk to the butter mixture until your preferred consistency is achieved
10. Spread the buttercream on the cupcake and serve.

Nutrition-Per Serving: Calories: 278Kcal, Total Fat: 12g, Carbs: 40g, Protein: 4g
Variation: Milk cream can be used instead of milk.

AIR FRYER CHOCOLATE CHIP COOKIES

Preparation Time: 10 minutes
Cooking Time: 5 minutes
Serving: 6

Ingredients
- ⅔ cup all-purpose flour
- ¼ tbsp baking soda
- ⅛ tbsp salt
- ⅓ cup brown sugar
- ¼ cup unsalted butter
- 2 tbsp white sugar
- 1 egg yolk
- ½ tbsp vanilla extract
- ½ semi-sweet chocolate chips.

Directions
1. Preheat the air fryer to 349°F.
2. In a bowl mix the flour, baking soda, and salt.
3. In a separate bowl add the brown sugar, butter, white sugar, egg, and vanilla extract.
4. Stir in the flour mixture to the butter mixture until the dough is well combined.
5. Add the chocolate chips to the dough and mix.
6. Scoop 2 spoonfuls of the dough, roll them into balls then flatten them into cookies.
7. Place the cookies in the air fryer and cook them for 5 minutes.
8. Transfer the cookies to a cooling rack and allow them to completely cool.
9. Serve and enjoy.

Nutrition-Per Serving: Calories: 268Kcal, Total Fat: 16g, Carbs: 34g, Protein: 4g
Variation: Bread flour can be used instead of all-purpose flour.

AIR FRYER CHOCOLATE CAKE

Preparation Time: 10 minutes
Cooking Time: 15 minutes
Serving: 4

Ingredients
- Cooking spray
- ¼ cup white sugar
- 3 ½ tbsp softened butter
- 1 egg, beaten
- 1 tbsp apricot jam
- 6 tbsp all-purpose flour
- 1 tbsp unsweetened cocoa chips
- Salt to taste

Directions
1. Preheat the air fryer to 319°F and spray a small pan with cooking spray.
2. Add sugar and butter to a bowl and mix using an electric mixer.
3. Add the egg and jam to the butter mixture and mix.
4. Sift the flour, cocoa chips, and salt over the butter mixture and thoroughly mix.
5. Pour all the batter into the pan and level with a spoon.
6. Cook the cake for 15 minutes.
7. Allow the cake to cool then serve.

Nutrition-Per Serving: Calories: 380Kcal, Total Fat: 27g, Carbs: 3g, Protein: 34g

Variation: Strawberry jam can be used instead of the apricot jam.

AIR FRYER APPLE FRITTERS

Preparation Time: 10 minutes

Cooking Time: 7 minutes

Serving: 6

Ingredients

- 1 cup all-purpose flour
- 2 tbsp sugar
- 1 tbsp baking powder
- ½ tbsp salt
- ½ tbsp ground cinnamon
- ¼ tbsp ground nutmeg
- 1 egg, beaten
- ⅓ cup milk
- 2 tbsp butter, melted
- ½ tbsp lemon juice
- 2 apples, diced

For the Cinnamon Glaze:

- ½ cup confectioners sugar
- 2 tbsp milk
- ½ tbsp ground cinnamon
- Pinch of salt

Directions

1. In a bowl, mix the flour, sugar, baking powder, salt, cinnamon, and nutmeg.

2. In a different bowl whisk the egg, milk, butter, and lemon juice.

3. Stir in the flour mixture into the egg mixture until well combined.

4. Fold the apple into the batter.

5. Scoop 2 spoonfuls of the batter and roll into the fritters.

6. Preheat the air fryer to 369°F

7. Place the apple fritters in the air fryer basket and c ook for 7 minutes.

8. Meanwhile, mix all the cinnamon glaze ingredients in a bowl.

9. Transfer the apple fritters to a wire rack and drizzle the cinnamon glaze on top.

10. Serve and enjoy.

Nutrition-Per Serving: Calories: 100Kcal, Total Fat: 3g, Carbs: 19g, Protein: 2g

Variation: Nutmeg can be replaced with mace.

AIR FRYER APPLE WEDGES

Preparation Time: 10 minutes

Cooking Time: 5 minutes

Serving: 6

Ingredients

- 1 cup graham cracker crumbs
- ¼ cup sugar
- 1 tbsp ground cinnamon
- 1 cup flour
- 3 eggs, beaten
- 3 apple, sliced into wedges
- Caramel sauce
-

Directions

1. Preheat the air fryer to 379°F.

2. In a bowl mix graham crackers crumbs, sugar, and cinnamon.

3. Place the flour and egg in 2 different bowls.

4. Dip the apple wedges in the flour, then into the egg, and finally in the graham crackers crumbs mixture.

5. Place the apple wedges in the air fryer and cook them for 5 minutes.

6. Serve the apple wedges with caramel sauce.

Nutrition-Per Serving: Calories: 237Kcal, Total Fat: 4g, Carbs: 43g, Protein: 5g

Variation: Graham crackers crumbs can be substituted with pretzels.

RECIPES FOR TWO

AIR FRYER TACO HOT DOGS

Preparation Time: 5 minutes
Cooking Time: 9 minutes
Serving: 2
Ingredients
2 hot dogs
1 tbsp taco seasoning mix
2 hot dog buns
⅓ cup guacamole
4 tbsp salsa
6 slices of pickled jalapeno
1 lemon, halved
Directions
1. Preheat the air fryer to 389°F.
2. Make 5 cuts on each hot dog then rub them with the taco seasoning.
3. Place the hot dogs in the air fryer basket and cook them for 5 minutes.
4. Place the hot dogs in the buns and cook for 4 minutes.
5. Top the hot dog with guacamole, salsa, and jalapeno.
6. Serve the taco hot dogs with lemon slices.
Nutrition-Per Serving: Calories: 380Kcal, Total Fat: 27g, Carbs: 3g, Protein: 34g
Variation: Favorite toppings can be used.

AIR FRYER LEMON PEPPER SHRIMP

Preparation Time: 5 minutes
Cooking Time: 6 minutes
Serving: 2
Ingredients
- 1 tbsp olive oil
- 1 lemon juice
- 1 tbsp lemon pepper
- ¼ tbsp paprika
- ¼ tbsp garlic powder
- 12 oz shrimp, peeled and deveined
- 1 lemon, sliced
- Parsley for topping
Directions
1. Preheat the air fryer to 399°F.
2. In a bowl mix olive oil, lemon juice, lemon pepper, paprika, and garlic powder until well combined.
3. Add the shrimp to the seasoning mixture and toss to coat.
4. Place the shrimp in an air fryer basket and cook for 6 minutes.
5. Serve the shrimp with lemon slices and sprinkle some parsley.
Nutrition-Per Serving: Calories: 215Kcal, Total Fat: 9g, Carbs: 13g, Protein: 29g
Variation: Favorite additional seasonings may be used.

AIR FRYER RICE

Preparation Time: 5 minutes
Cooking Time: 16 minutes
Serving: 2

Ingredients

- 2 tbsp soy sauce
- 2 tbsp sriracha sauce
- 2 cups cooked rice
- 1 tbsp sesame oil
- 1 tbsp water
- 2 tbsp vegetable oil
- Salt and black pepper to taste
- 1 egg, beaten
- 1 cup peas and carrot

Directions

1. Preheat the air fryer to 349°F.
2. In a bowl, whisk the soy sauce and sriracha sauce then set aside.
3. In a separate bowl mix the rice, sesame oil, water, vegetable oil, salt, and pepper.
4. Transfer the rice mixture to a cake pan and place it in the air fryer basket.
5. Cook the rice for 10 minutes stirring halfway through the cooking time.
6. Pour the egg over the rice and cook for 4 minutes.
7. Stir in the peas and carrots to the rice then cook for 2 minutes.
8. Plate the rice and pour the sauce over.
9. Serve and enjoy.

Nutrition-Per Serving: Calories: 392Kcal, Total Fat: 15g, Carbs: 55g, Protein: 11g

Variation: Favorite sauces can be used.

AIR FRYER MASHED POTATO BALLS

Preparation Time: 10 minutes
Cooking Time: 12 minutes
Serving: 2

Ingredients

- ¼ cup bread crumbs
- ½ tbsp parmesan cheese, grated
- ¼ tbsp dried parsley
- ⅛ tbsp garlic powder
- ⅛ tbsp black pepper
- ⅛ tbsp salt
- ⅛ cup aquafaba
- 1 tbsp nutritional yeast
- 1 cup cold mashed potatoes
- Olive oil spray

For garnishing: grated parmesan cheese and scallions

Directions

1. In a bowl mix the bread crumbs, parmesan, parsley, garlic powder, pepper, and salt.
2. Place the aquafaba and the yeast on 2 different bowls.
3. Scoop 2 spoonfuls of the mashed potatoes and roll them into balls.
4. Coat the balls with yeast, then dip them in the aquafaba and finally coat them with the bread crumbs mixture.
5. Preheat the air fryer to 389°F and grease the air fryer basket with cooking spray.
6. Place the potato balls in the air fryer basket and spritz them with cooking spray.
7. Cook the potato balls for 12 minutes shaking the basket 3 times during the cooking.
8. Garnish the potato balls with parmesan and scallions then serve.

Nutrition-Per Serving: Calories: 95Kcal, Total Fat: 1g, Carbs: 18g, Protein: 5g

Variation: Parmesan cheese can be replaced with favorite cheese.

AIR FRYER MAC AND CHEESE

Preparation Time: 20 minutes
Cooking Time: 6 minutes
Serving: 2
Ingredients

- 1 (7.5 oz)box macaroni and cheese
- 2 bacon slices
- ½ cup broccoli florets
- 1 egg
- ⅓ cup shredded cheddar cheese
- ¼ cup french fried onions

Directions

1. Cook the macaroni and cheese according to the packaging directions.
2. Meanwhile, cook the bacon in a skillet over medium heat for 10 minutes.
3. Stir in the broccoli to the mac and cheese during the last 2 minutes of cooking.
4. Cut the bacon into small pieces and mix with the egg in a bowl.
5. Stir in the bacon mixture to the mac and cheese mixture.
6. Preheat the air fryer to 399°F and spray the muffin cups with cooking spray.
7. Fill the muffin cups with 2 spoonfuls of the mac and cheese mixture then top with cheddar cheese and fried onions.
8. Cook the mac and cheese bites for 8 minutes.
9. Let the mac and cheese bite cool for 3 minutes then use tongs to remove them from the cups.
10. Serve and enjoy.

Nutrition-Per Serving: Calories: 55Kcal, Total Fat: 3g, Carbs: 6g, Protein: 3g
Variation: Broccoli can be replaced with preferred veggies.

AIR FRYER BLACKENED CHICKEN BREAST

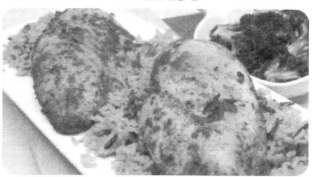

Preparation Time: 10 minutes
Cooking Time: 20 minutes
Serving: 2
Ingredients

2 tbsp paprika
1 tbsp ground thyme
1 tbsp cumin
½ tbsp cayenne pepper
½ tbsp onion powder
½ tbsp black pepper
¼ tbsp salt
2 tbsp vegetable oil
2 chicken breast halves, skinless and boneless
Cooked rice and broccoli
Parsley for topping

Directions

1. In a bowl mix paprika, thyme, cumin, cayenne pepper, onion powder, black pepper, and salt.
2. Coat the chicken breast with oil then rub them with the seasoning mixture.
3. Allow the chicken to marinate for 5 minutes.
4. Preheat the air fryer to 359°F.
5. Place the chicken breast in the air fryer basket and cook for 20 minutes. Flip the chicken after 10 minutes of cooking.
6. Serve the chicken with cooked rice and broccoli and top with parsley.

Nutrition-Per Serving: Calories: 432Kcal, Total Fat: 10g, Carbs: 3g, Protein: 79g
Variation: The seasonings may be adjusted to fit your preference.

AIR FRYER SALMON CAKE WITH SRIRACHA MAYO

Preparation Time: 15 minutes
Cooking Time: 8 minutes
Serving: 2
Ingredients
For Sriracha Mayo:
- ⅛ cup mayonnaise
- ½ tbsp sriracha

For the Salmon Cakes:
- ½ lb salmon fillets, skinless
- ¼ cup almond flour
- 1 egg, beaten
- ¾ tbsp old bay seasoning
- 1 green onion, chopped
- Cooking spray

Directions
1. In a bowl, prepare the sriracha mayo by whisking mayonnaise and sriracha. Refrigerate until ready to use.
2. Add 1 tablespoon of sriracha mayo, salmon, almond flour, egg, seasoning, and ¾ of the onion to a food processor and pulse until they are well combined.
3. Make 4 patties from the salmon mixture and refrigerate them for 15 minutes.
4. Preheat the air fryer to 389°F and spray the air fryer basket with cooking spray.
5. Spritz the salmon patties with cooking spray and place them in the air fryer basket.
6. Cook the cakes for 8 minutes.
7. Serve the salmon with the remaining sriracha mayo and green onions.
Nutrition-Per Serving: Calories: 340Kcal, Total Fat: 25g, Carbs: 4g, Protein: 26g
Variation: Red onions can be used instead of green onions.

AIR FRYER LAVA CAKES

Preparation Time: 10 minutes
Cooking Time: 10 minutes
Serving: 2
Ingredients
- Cooking spray
- ½ cup semi-sweet chocolate chips
- 4 tbsp butter
- 2 eggs, beaten
- 1 tbsp vanilla extract
- ¼ tbsp salt
- 3 tbsp all-purpose flour
- ½ cup powdered sugar

For the Nutella Filling:
- 2 tbsp Nutella
- 1 tbsp softened butter
- 1 tbsp powdered

Directions
1. Preheat the air fryer to 369°F and spray the ramekins with cooking spray.
2. Add chocolate chips and butter to a bowl then melt them in the microwave.
3. Stir the eggs, vanilla, salt, flour, powdered sugar into the butter mixture.
4. In a separate bowl mix the Nutella filling ingredients until they are well combined.
5. Fill the ramekins with the half-full batter and a Nutella filling at the center. Cover the Nutella filling with the remaining batter.
6. Place the lava cakes in an air fryer and cook them for 10 minutes.
7. Remove the cakes from the air fryer and flip them over a plate.
8. Allow the cake to cool for 5 minutes then serve.
Nutrition-Per Serving: Calories: 776Kcal, Total Fat: 50g, Carbs: 77g, Protein: 10g
Variation: maple syrup can be used instead of vanilla extract.

AIR FRYER PORK CHOPS WITH BRUSSELS SPROUTS

Preparation Time: 10 minutes
Cooking Time: 10 minutes
Serving: 1
Ingredients

- 8 oz pork chops, bone-in
- Cooking spray
- ⅛ tbsp salt
- ½ tbsp black pepper
- 1 tbsp olive oil
- 1 tbsp maple syrup
- 1 tbsp Dijon mustard
- 6 oz Brussels sprouts

Directions

1. Mist the pork chops with cooking spray and season them with salt and ¼ tablespoon pepper.
2. In a bowl whisk oil, maple syrup, mustard, and remaining pepper.
3. Add the Brussels in the Dijon mixture and toss to coat.
4. Preheat the air fryer to 399°F.
5. Place the pork chops on one side of the air fryer basket and the Brussels on the other side.
6. Cook the pork chops for 10 minutes.
7. Serve and enjoy.

Nutrition-Per Serving: Calories: 337Kcal, Total Fat: 11g, Carbs: 21g, Protein: 39g
Variation: Dijon mustard can be replaced with mayonnaise.

AIR FRYER MAPLE SAGE SQUASH

Preparation Time: 10 minutes
Cooking Time: 12 minutes
Serving: 1
Ingredients

⅛ lb butternut squash, peeled and cut into 1-inch pieces
1 tbsp olive oil
½ tbsp salt
A handful of sage leaves
½ tbsp maple syrup
2 tbsp pomegranate seeds

Directions

1. Add the squash, ½ tablespoon oil, and salt to a bowl and toss to coat.
2. Preheat the air fryer to 374°F.
3. Place the squash in an air fryer basket and cook for 7 minutes.
4. Meanwhile, rub the sage with the remaining oil.
5. Stir in the sage to the squash and cook for 5 minutes.
6. Transfer the squash to a bowl and drizzle with maple syrup then toss to coat.
7. Plate the squash and sprinkle pomegranate seed over.
8. Serve and enjoy.

Nutrition-Per Serving: Calories: 685Kcal, Total Fat: 63g, Carbs: 33g, Protein: 3g
Variation: Preferred squash can be used.

SMOKY PORK TENDERLOIN WITH BUTTERNUT SQUASH

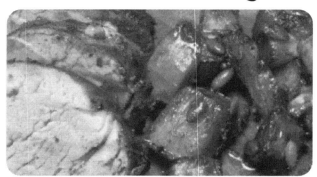

Preparation Time: 10 minutes

Cooking Time: 17 minutes

Serving: 1

Ingredients

- ¼ lb pork tenderloin
- ½ tbsp smoked paprika
- Salt and black pepper to taste
- ⅛ tbsp ground cumin
- ½ tbsp canola oil
- 3 oz butternut squash
- ⅛ cup cider vinegar
- ¾ tbsp honey
- ¼ tbsp Dijon mustard
- 1 thyme sprig
- ¼ tbsp unsalted butter, melted

Directions

1. Preheat the air fryer to 399°F.

2. Sprinkle the pork with paprika, salt, pepper, and cumin then rub to coat.

3. Heat ¼ tablespoon oil in a skillet over medium heat then brown the pork on both sides for 4 minutes.

4. Add the butternut and remaining oil to a bowl and toss to coat.

5. Air fry the butternut for 5 minutes.

6. Stir the pork into the butternut and cook for 8 minutes.

7. Remove the pork and butternut from the air fryer and let stand for 5 minutes.

8. Meanwhile, mix the vinegar, honey, mustard, thyme, and salt in a saucepan.

9. Cook the sauce over medium heat until thickened.

10. Stir the butter into the sauce and remove it from heat. Discard the thyme sprig.

11. Plate the pork and butternut then drizzle the sauce.

12. Serve and enjoy.

Nutrition-Per Serving: Calories: 390Kcal, Total Fat: 13g, Carbs: 44g, Protein: 25g

Variation: Dijon mustard can be replaced with mayonnaise.

AIR FRYER MEATLOAF

Preparation Time: 10 minutes

Cooking Time: 25 minutes

Serving: 1

Ingredients

- Cooking spray
- ¼ lb lean ground beef
- 1 egg, beaten
- 1 tbsp bread crumbs
- 1 finely chopped onion
- ¼ tbsp chopped thyme
- Salt and black pepper
- 1 small mushroom, chopped
- 2 tbsp buffalo wings sauce

Directions

1. Preheat the air fryer to 391°F and spray a baking pan with cooking spray.

2. In a bowl mix, the beef, egg, breadcrumbs, onion, thyme, salt, and pepper.

3. Transfer the beef mixture to the pan and level the top with a spoon.

4. Press the mushroom into the beef mixture and spritz the top with cooking spray.

5. Transfer the pan to the air fryer basket and cook for 25 minutes.

6. Allow the meatloaf to cool then slice it.

7. Serve the meatloaf with buffalo wings sauce.

Nutrition-Per Serving: Calories: 296Kcal, Total Fat: 19g, Carbs: 6g, Protein: 25g

Variation: Breadcrumbs may be substituted with oatmeal.

Air Fried Sesame-Crusted Cod with Snap Peas

Preparation Time: 10 minutes
Cooking Time: 16 minutes
Serving: 1
Ingredients
1 cod fillet
½ tbsp vegetable oil
Salt and black pepper to taste
1 tbsp butter
½ tbsp sesame seeds
1 ½ oz sugar snap peas
1 garlic clove, sliced
2 orange wedges

Directions
1. Preheat the air fryer to 399°F and grease the air fryer basket with vegetable oil.
2. Dry the salmon with a paper towel then season it with salt and pepper.
3. In a bowl mix the butter and sesame seeds.
4. In a separate bowl add the peas, garlic, and ½ of the butter mixture and toss to mix.
5. Place the peas in an air fryer and cook for 10 minutes. Shake the basket 2 times during the cooking.
6. Transfer the snap peas to a bowl. Keep the snap peas warm.
7. Brush the fillet with the remaining butter mixture then place it in the air fryer.
8. Cook the fillet for 6 minutes
9. Serve the fillet with the peas and orange wedges.
Nutrition-Per Serving: Calories: 364Kcal, Total Fat: 15g, Carbs: 23g, Protein: 31g
Variation: Vegetable oil can be replaced with cooking spray.

Brussels Sprouts with Bacon and Maple Syrup

Preparation Time: 10 minutes
Cooking Time: 10 minutes
Serving: 1

Ingredients
- 2 tbsp avocado oil
- 2 tbsp maple syrup
- 1 tbsp apple cider vinegar
- Salt and black pepper
- ¼ lb Brussels sprouts, trimmed
- 1 slice bacon, cut into small pieces

Directions
1. Add oil, maple syrup, vinegar, salt, and pepper to a bowl and mix.
2. Stir in the Brussel sprouts and bacon to the marinade.
3. Preheat the air fryer to 349°F.
4. Transfer the Brussels sprouts and bacon to an air fryer.
5. Cook the Brussels and bacon for 10 minutes stirring halfway through cooking.
6. Serve and enjoy.

Nutrition-Per Serving: Calories: 528Kcal, Total Fat: 39g, Carbs: 42g, Protein: 8g

Variation: Red wine vinegar can be used in place of apple cider vinegar

AIR FRYER CHEESE STUFFED MUSHROOM

Preparation Time: 5 minutes
Cooking Time: 8 minutes
Serving: 1

Ingredients
- 2 oz fresh Portobello mushroom
- 1 oz cream cheese
- 1 tbsp parmesan cheese, shredded
- ½ tbsp sharp cheddar cheese, shredded
- ½ tbsp white cheddar cheese, shredded
- 1 tbsp Worcestershire sauce
- 1 garlic clove, minced
- Salt and black pepper to taste
- Parsley for garnishing

Directions
1. Cut off the mushroom stem and remove much of the mushroom flesh.
2. In a bowl mix cream cheese, parmesan, cheddar cheeses, Worcestershire sauce, garlic, salt, and pepper.
3. Preheat the air fryer to 369°F.
4. Stuff the mushrooms with the cheese mixture and place them in the air fryer basket.
5. Cook the stuffed mushroom for 8 minutes.
6. Allow the mushrooms to cool.
7. Sprinkle parsley over the mushrooms and serve.

Nutrition-Per Serving: Calories: 116Kcal, Total Fat: 7g, Carbs: 3g, Protein: 8g

Variation: Preferred cheeses can be used

AIR FRYER SALMON AND ASPARAGUS

Preparation Time: 5 minutes
Cooking Time: 8 minutes
Serving: 1

Ingredients
- ¾ tbsp lemon juice
- ½ tbsp olive oil
- 1 tbsp fresh dill, chopped
- 1 tbsp fresh parsley, chopped
- Salt and pepper to taste
- 1 salmon filet
- 1 bunch asparagus

Directions
1. In a bowl mix lemon juice, olive oil, dill, parsley, salt, and pepper.
2. Coat the salmon with ¾ dill mixture.
3. Stir the asparagus into the remaining dill mixture.
4. Preheat the air fryer to 399°F.
5. Place the asparagus at the bottom of the air fryer basket and layer the salmon on top.
6. Cook the salmon for 8 minutes.
7. Plate and serve.

Nutrition-Per Serving: Calories: 391Kcal, Total Fat: 20g, Carbs: 9g, Protein: 48g

Variation: Preferred herbs can be used.

AIR FRYER COOKING CHART

VEGETABLES

	QUALITY	TEMP	TIME(min)		QUALITY	TEMP	TIME (min)
Asparagus	1 Inch slices	400°F	5	Parsnips	½ inch chunk	400°F	15
Beets	Whole	400°F	40	Peppers	1 inch chunk	400°F	15
Broccoli	Florets	400°F	6	Potatoes	1 inch chunk	400°F	12
Brussels sprouts	Halved	380°F	15	Baby potatoes	1 ½ lb	400°F	15
Carrots	½ inch slices	380°F	15	Squash	½ inch	400°F	12
Cauliflower	Florets	400°F	12	Sweet Potatoes		380°F	35
Corn on the Cob		390°F	6	Tomatoes	Halved	350°F	10
Eggplant	1 ½ inch cubes	400°F	15	Cherry Tomatoes		400°F	4
Fennel	quartered	370°F	15	Zucchini	½ inch sticks	400°F	12
Green Beans		400°F	5				
Kale Leaves		250°F	12				
Mushrooms	¼ inch slices	400°F	5				
Onions	sliced	400°F	10				

FISH AND SEAFOOD

	QUALITY	TEMP	TIME(min)		QUALITY	TEMP	TIME (min)
Calamari	8 Oz	400°F	4	Tuna steak		400°F	7- 10
Fish Fillet	1 inch 8 oz	400°F	10	Scallops		400°F	5-7
Salmon Fillet	6 oz	380°F	12	Shrimp		400°F	5
Sword Fish		400°F	10				
Sea Beam							

POULTRY

	QUALITY	TEMP	TIME(min)		QUALITY	TEMP	TIME (min)
Chicken breast	(bone in)1 ¼ lb	370°F	25	Chicken legs	Bone in)1.75lb	380°F	30
Chicken breast	Boneless 4 oz	380°F	12	Wings	2 lb	400°F	12
Drumsticks	2 ½ lb	370°F	20	Game hen	Halved) 2 lb	390°F	75
Thighs	(Bone in) 2 lb	380°F	22	Tenders		360°F	10
Thighs	(Boneless)1.5lb	380°F	20				

BEEF

	QUALITY	TEMP	TIME(min)		QUALITY	TEMP	TIME (min)
Burger	4 oz	370°F	16-20	Rib eye	1 inch 8oz	400°F	10-15
Frank Steak	1.5 lbs	400°F	18	Sirloin Steaks	1 inch 12 oz	400°F	9-15
London Broil	2 lbs	400°F	12	Eye round roast	4 lv	390°F	45-55
Meatballs	1 inch	380°F	20-28				

PORK AND LAMB

	QUALITY	TEMP	TIME(min)		QUALITY	TEMP	TIME (min)
Loin	2 lb	360°F	55	Sausage		380°F	15
Pork chops	1 inch 6.5 oz	400°F	12	Lamb Chops	1 inch	400°F	12
Tenderloin	1 lb	370°F	15	Rack of Lamb	2 lb	380°F	22
Bacon		400°F	7				

OTHERS

	QUALITY	TEMP	TIME(min)		QUALITY	TEMP	TIME (min)
Egg rolls	7	390°F	5	muffins	10	360°F	12
pizza		390°F	10	Soft fruits	4 cups	320°F	3 -5
Cake	8 inch pan	320°F	25	Hard fruit	4 cups	320°F	5- 10

AIR FRYER CONVERSION TABLE

VOLUME EQUIVALENT (LIQUID)

us standard	us standard Oz	metric(approx.)
2 tbsp	1 fl.oz	30 ml
¼ cup	2 fl.oz	60 ml
½ cup	4 fl.oz	120 ml
1 cup	8 fl.oz	240 ml
1 1/2 cup	12 fl.oz	355 ml
2 cups/ 1 pint	36 fl.oz	475 ml
4 cups/ 1 quart	32 fl.oz	1 L
1 gallon	128 fl.oz	4 L

VOLUME EQUIVALENT (DRY)

US STANDARD	METRIC (Approx.)
1/8 tbsp	0.5 ml
¼ tbsp	1 ml
½ tbsp	2 ml
¾ tbsp	5 ml
1 tbsp	15 ml
1 Tbsp	59 ml
1/8 cup	79 ml
¼ cup	119 ml
½ cup	156 ml
¾ cup	177 ml
1 cup	235 ml
2 cups/ 1 pint	475 ml
3 cups	700 ml
4 cups	1 L
½ gallon	2 L
1 gallon	4 L

TEMPERATURES

FAHRENHEIT (F)	CELCIUS (C)
250	120
300	150
325	165
350	180
375	190
400	200
425	220
450	230

WEIGHT EQUIVALENT

US STANDARD	METRIC (Approx.)
½ ounce	15g
1 ounce	30g
2 ounce	60g
4 ounce	115g
8 ounce	225g
12 ounce	340g
16 ounce/ 1 pound	455g

Printed in Great Britain
by Amazon